Depression, Anger, Sadness

Teens Write About Facing Difficult Emotions

By Youth Communication

Edited by Al Desetta

True Stories by Teens

Depression, Anger, Sadness

EXECUTIVE EDITORS
Keith Hefner and Laura Longhine

CONTRIBUTING EDITORS
Nora McCarthy, Andrea Estepa, Hope Vanderberg, Rachel Blustain,
Duffy Cohen, Sheila Feeney, Marie Glancy, and Clarence Haynes

LAYOUT & DESIGN
Efrain Reyes, Jr. and Jeff Faerber

COVER ART
Patricia Battles

For reprint information, please contact Youth Communication.

ISBN 978-1-933939-79-7

Second, Expanded Edition

Printed in the United States of America

Youth Communication ®
New York, New York
www.youthcomm.org

Table of Contents

Introduction

In the opening story of *Depression, Anger, Sadness*, Alina Serrano starts feeling sad, angry, and confused during her first year in high school. Her parents are getting divorced and her house feels "like a ticking bomb, ready to explode and destroy everyone in it." Depression overtakes her, transforming her into "a totally different person."

"I became self-conscious and obsessive, trying to figure out how others were reacting to my every word, move, and action," Alina writes. "I spent too many nights crying for a sorrow I felt in my heart that nobody, including myself, could explain."

By age 15, when she's a sophomore in high school, Alina is so depressed that suicide seems the only way out. But then she gets "in the ring" with her depression and starts to fight back. She sees a counselor and begins to understand how her sorrow is linked with her past.

"The counseling process helped me understand what depression was and how it affected me," Alina writes. "And, most of all, how to deal with it."

Depression, Anger, Sadness collects 16 true stories by teens, who write candidly and courageously about facing difficult emotions and what they did to try to help themselves. For example, Alina learns to think in more positive ways when situations get her down. She writes in a journal. She plays handball. And she opens up to her family and close friends about her fears, anxieties, and pain.

"I knew they couldn't shield me from depression," Alina writes, "but they could help me fight it." By telling her support group how she feels and what she needs, Alina begins to recover. While she still struggles with depression, she has learned strategies to keep it under control and no longer feels alone.

This book includes interviews with therapists and youth workers, who offer practical advice about identifying depression, dealing with sadness and loss, and how and when to seek outside help. And in their stories, the writers address a wide range of emotional issues and challenges. Griffin Kinard uses writing to release his emotions and help deal with the pain of losing loved ones. Magda Czubak is devastated when a boy she's desperately in love with starts going out with her best friend. She throws herself into new interests and activities to overcome her depression. Dina Spanbock spends three months at a treatment center, where she finds a supportive community of other teens who know what she's going through.

In "Dealing With It," Hazel Tesoro leaves foster care to live on her own, thinking she's closed the door forever on a painful past. "I soon found out that those gates don't shut that easily," Hazel writes. "No matter where I went, I felt judged, alone, and angry. I couldn't simply 'get over' my past, as people kept telling me to do."

Hazel gradually gains more emotional stability, as do almost all of the writers in this book. They face their problems and reach inside themselves to draw on their strength and resilience.

In the final story, Hattie Rice uses the tools she learns in a special workshop for teens to make changes in her life. Although she's had a lot to deal with, Hattie also realizes that her own attitude is holding her back from growing as a person. Instead of blaming the past or getting stuck in it, she starts to focus on her positive qualities.

"I've uncovered some interesting things about myself," Hattie writes. "I've realized that I'm stronger than I thought I was. I feel inspired to work on other aspects of my life that bother me. Maybe it is possible for me to be happier day to day."

In the following stories, names have been changed: *Out of the Shadows, My Brother Kareem.*

Melanie Leong

Fighting the Monster Inside Me

By Alina Serrano

My dear friend,

Hey, what's up, love? I heard you've been feeling bad. I can see it in your eyes.

I know what you're going through. I've been there—that's why I can see it and others can't. You feel lonely, heartbroken, angry, right? Well, let me tell you—you're not alone. You never were.

I'm going to take this time to tell you about my experience. Maybe the same one you're going through right now. You feel like you've hit rock bottom. But you have to fight. The problem is, you don't know who or what.

You and me, we've got the same enemy. The one who lurks in our everyday thoughts. Who attacks us with no warning. This enemy is not a person or a thing, but a force. I choose to call it Mr. Hyde because it is the monster that lives within me.

Dr. Jekyll is who I am when I'm happy, when I feel loved and important. But Dr. Jekyll and Mr. Hyde used to switch places on me, spontaneously, without warning. All of a sudden, I would turn sad, angry, moody. That was Mr. Hyde taking me over, transforming me into a totally different person.

I'm going to let you in on a little secret. Mr. Hyde's real name is depression. By finding that out, I learned how to beat him. And so will you.

I still recall when I first started feeling helpless, lonely, sad, angry, and confused. At that point in my life, I was going through many dilemmas. I was in my first year of high school. My school responsibilities were getting greater at the same time that my parents were getting divorced.

My mother, who helped me with all my problems, was depressed herself. My father was getting edgier and seemed more out of control. It got to the point where even my older sister, my only source of relief, didn't have all the answers. She started losing her cool, too. My house felt like a ticking bomb, ready to explode and destroy everyone in it. That's when Mr. Hyde moved in and became my sworn enemy.

My teenage life was turning upside down. Instead of chilling with my friends after school, I would hurry home and stay cooped up in my house all day. In spite of all the tension there, it was the only place I felt safe. In my house, I didn't have to put on an act for anyone that everything was OK.

My doorbell would ring and it would be my friend asking if I wanted to take a walk or just chill. I would always make up an excuse, such as feeling sick or being too busy with my homework.

That wasn't like me. In the past I would always hang out with my family and friends with a smile on my face, no matter what situation we were in. I always loved to listen to music and dance along with it. But these things no longer brought me joy.

Even though I was an honors student, I felt like nothing. Even though I had the love of my family, my best friend, and occasional boyfriends, I felt like nothing.

People who know me have always said that I'm feisty and a fighter. My mother tells me I'm "like an ax and a machete" because I always stand up for what I believe in. Still, I couldn't shake the feeling of being a nothing.

Depression does that to you. It had me looking towards nothing, feeling nothing. My head was full of negative thoughts. I became self-conscious and obsessive, trying to figure out how others were reacting to my every word, move, and action.

I was always asking myself, "Do people step all over me?" I was always on point, ready to fight anyone and anything for no reason. I got into fights and arguments just to prove to myself that I wasn't a punk, a nobody. It was exhausting.

I became self-conscious and obsessive, trying to figure out how others were reacting to my every word, move, and action.

It was as if Mr. Hyde was getting stronger and, in the process, taking away all my best qualities, like being kind, loyal to my loved ones, optimistic, intelligent, and determined to do what was right.

I didn't like who I was becoming, so I was mean to myself. I felt I deserved nothing but unhappiness. I spent too many nights crying for a sorrow I felt in my heart that nobody, including myself, could explain. I know you feel that way too.

Let me tell you, by my second year of high school I was at my worst. I was only 15 and I was waiting to die. Mr. Hyde was trying to take away my quality of never giving up. It felt like suicide would be my only escape.

One day I was sitting at my kitchen table, trying to work on my geometry homework, but unable to concentrate. I looked up and saw a big kitchen knife. I stared at it in a daze, thinking, "I can cut my wrists now and never feel this bad again."

I got up from the table and put the knife away and left the

kitchen. A couple of days passed before I told anybody. I had never felt that way before and it scared me very much. I had always felt my life was precious and Mr. Hyde was even trying to take that away. He was determined to completely take over, but I finally decided I wouldn't let him. Suicide isn't a solution. It isn't for anyone, not me and not you.

So, guess what I did? I got in the ring with Mr. Hyde. I started to fight back, because I wasn't going to let him win. No, señor, not me, not ever. And he isn't going to win with you, either!

I fought back by going to get help. A friend from school introduced me to a counselor who I will call Angel, because he has been mine. At first I felt weird talking to him. I felt he didn't need to hear my problems. But I also felt I had nothing to lose, so I started seeing Angel on a regular basis.

I spent too many nights crying for a sorrow I felt in my heart that nobody, including myself, could explain.

I had never thought about getting counseling before, because I thought a therapist wouldn't really care. But Angel showed me he did care, just by saying the right things or giving me a hug when I needed one. He made it easy to talk. He showed me he understood and was there to help. He won my trust simply by being sincere and caring.

I know you may be thinking, the way I used to, "What can a stranger do for me?" The fact that he was a stranger actually made things easier. It eased my concerns about the impression I gave off. I didn't worry about him judging me because he didn't really know me.

The first thing Angel ever asked me was who I loved the most. I responded by saying, "My mother, my sister, my brother, my father." He looked at me and said, "Funny, you never mentioned you." I had spent so much time condemning myself in every possible way that I was unable to give myself some of the caring that I have for others.

Angel made me see that I had to start helping myself. He taught me to respect and appreciate myself, to make myself comfortable with "me."

With Angel's help, I realized that much of my sorrow came from my past. The counseling process helped me understand what depression was and how it affected me. And, most of all, how to deal with it.

Angel helped me learn to think more positive when situations got me down. I would write in a journal every day and look for activities that would help me express my feelings. I started playing handball to keep myself active and sane. I even went on medication for a while.

After I started talking to Angel, I told my family and my close friends about the struggle I was having—about the fears, the anxiety, the insecurities and pain. I knew they couldn't shield me from depression, but they could help me fight it.

After that, Mr. Hyde had to deal with an entire group, not just one person. My point is, you can't be alone on this. You need partners, a team. My family and best friend made up my support group. Every one of them had a way of making me feel better. My mother would hold me and hug me so tight when I felt bad that I felt secure in her arms.

My sister reassured me when I went to her with my everyday worries. She would say, "No, you didn't look stupid in front of them," or "Cry it out, it'll be better that way."

My best friend would go with me to the park to run and scream when I felt I needed to let my frustrations out.

Even my father, who never expresses his emotions, told me one day that even though he loved me and my siblings the same, he always had a special bond with me. Then he took me shopping for a new outfit. That had the biggest impact on me. My father, who is Mr. Tough Guy, took time out to make me feel better. For that, I love him in a special way.

Last, but not least, my brother, my twin, only had to give me a smile or act silly to make my day brighter.

Telling the people closest to me how I felt and what I needed made our relationships stronger and better. It put us on a new level of understanding. For instance, when I secluded myself, they knew I wasn't just being cranky. They understood it was a warning sign of Mr. Hyde's arrival. They stood by me during my hardest times and I will always be grateful to all of them.

Things started to turn around. I started to feel good about myself again. When I was a junior, I was inducted into the National Honor Society. Last spring, I graduated from high school and now I'm in college. These accomplishments have reminded me that I am somebody, and an important person at that.

I got in the ring with Mr. Hyde. I started to fight back.

I feel like myself again. I can dance and chill all day without feeling bad. I don't feel the need to pick fights anymore. I don't have to prove to anyone that I am not a punk or a herb. I feel more at ease with myself. I still have days when I feel like Mr. Hyde has just punched me in the face. But I always knock him out before he can do too much damage.

As I write this, I get the butterflies—just like when you are getting ready to fight or challenge someone. In a way, I'm still fighting, always will be. But I'm not alone and you aren't either. I've learned how to control my sad days and what to do to make them better, and you can too.

As for my long letter, I'll end it now by telling you that I'm not writing this so you can feel pity or compassion for me. I just want to let you know that I have felt your pain and that you are not alone.

This is what I ask of you: to fight back with whatever tools you have, to prove to Mr. Hyde that he isn't stronger than you. If you need a little help, just remind him of his experience with me. Go and speak to the people who you know can help. Look for them in your family, at your school, anywhere.

If you do that, Mr. Hyde is sure to succumb enough to let you start doing your thing. Always remember to keep your head up, stay strong, and honor yourself.

Peace.

Your friend,

Alina

Alina was 18 when she wrote this story.
She attended Hunter College.

Kaisha Jones

Clean and Kind of Sober

By Antwaun Garcia

When I was a kid, I noticed how family members picked up a cigarette whenever they felt stress or got mad. My mom would hand me her boggy (cigarette) and tell me to flush it down the toilet. One day, when I was 9, I closed the bathroom door and smoked it.

I figured that if my parents saw me smoking they'd laugh, like parents do when they watch a little girl walk in high heels impersonating her mother. But soon I used cigarettes the same way my parents did—to feel better.

When I was 10, my life got stressful. My friend Ricky died in a fire, and I went into foster care, moving to my aunt's house in Queens, because my mom was using drugs.

When I couldn't read a book my aunt gave me, thought about how my dad used to hit my mom, or wondered what my mom was doing on the streets, I couldn't wait to smoke a cigarette. Sometimes I even sneaked a little alcohol. At family parties my grandma had let us try it, and it made me feel loose.

Then, when I was 13, my best friend, Jarrel, killed himself. After he died, I drank a bunch of Bacardi and sat out on my terrace crying, confused and lost, thinking about my friends' deaths, not being with my parents or brothers, and feeling isolated instead of loved.

I felt completely alone. I doubted anyone could understand me or all that I had gone through.

After Jarrel died, I wrote many poems about guilt, death and anger. I found that writing helped me vent emotions. But the next year, when I got to high school, my boys put me on to something even better: smoking weed. I loved it from the first.

We cut class, went to my boy's crib and smoked about four blunts. I took a mean pull, and after the second pull I didn't want to pass it around.

In my first two years of high school, I cut class over 300 times and had a 55 average. I liked smoking so much because I never thought about my past or my life when I was high. I just thought about food and what I was going to do when I get home.

I felt completely alone. I doubted anyone could understand me or all that I had gone through.

I smoked mostly by myself, because when I was smoking with my friends, I would come out with thoughts that I later regretted sharing. I didn't want my boys to know me too well. By 15, I was lighting up by myself in a park far from my neighborhood.

By 17, I was also drinking a lot, taking Bacardi or Hennessy to school in water bottles or drinking after school in a park. I felt lonely, frustrated, angry and helpless.

I thought it best to drink alone so I didn't show anyone my sadness or get in trouble. When I drank I wanted to fight. If I had liqs in me, I didn't care who the dude was, I threw the hands.

With every fight, the anger of my childhood ran through my body. I didn't like who I was, but fighting, drinking, smoking and writing were the only ways I knew of to deal with my emotions.

Then, when I was 18, I met a girl in my high school. She was a Dominican mami, a natural beauty, intelligent, loved to laugh, and had a beautiful smile. We had two classes together and eventually started dating.

Together we went shopping, to movies and amusement parks, and on picnics in Flushing Meadows. At night we would sit in a park and talk for hours, or bug out in hotels, ordering Pizza Hut and watching movies and having bugged out pillow fights. We couldn't get enough of one another.

I learned how to talk about my feelings rather than hide from them.

But my habits started to affect our relationship. Every time I drank, the anger I bottled in came out. On the phone, she would hear me breathing hard and ask, "Antwaun, are you OK?" I'd tell her about a fight I had, usually because I was smoking or drinking.

She realized that smoking and drinking brought out the demon in me, which we were both scared of. My girl would cry because she felt helpless to calm or console me, and I'd get mad at myself for putting her through pain.

Finally one day she told me, "Antwaun, you know I love you, right?"

"Yes!" I replied.

"I love you so much that it hurts. So you have to choose — your habits or me."

I didn't know what to say but I was thinking, "Antwaun, you're losing someone important, and for what? Choose her before you lose her!" So I told her I would stop.

I never completely stopped drinking. (My girl sometimes drank, too, and we'd have a few drinks together.) But I made a major effort to keep my cups under control. Smoking I stopped completely, because I didn't need to escape my reality when I was with her.

As I let her get to know me, she helped me let out some of the feelings I kept inside. To help her understand why I was so angry, I told her about my past.

We talked for hours about each other's pasts, even though her past wasn't like mine. She listened to me, so I felt at ease coming out with everything. I learned how to talk about my feelings rather than hide from them.

Whenever I started to cry, she would tell me, "You don't have to tell me if you're not ready," because she knew I hated crying. I would hold my head back and cover my eyes, and she would hug me and say, "It's OK to cry. I'm here. Everything is fine."

Whatever I didn't tell her about myself, she read in my articles. She kept a book of all my articles and saved them next to her journal and baby pictures. I also kept writing down all my emotions to prevent that feeling of pressure from holding too much in.

With my girl's help, I became more focused in school and my life started to look clearer. I was good.

After two years, my girl became depressed due to family issues. Then she moved away. We broke up in January '04. After that, I fell into a deep depression that lasted for months. I felt alone and lost. I had no clue of what I wanted to do in life.

I started drinking and smoking again, fell off in school and didn't wash because I wanted to look like I felt: dirty and pathetic. I was always mad. I stopped writing and let my pain eat at me.

My cravings for fast food became real serious, too. Whenever I went to Micky D's I ordered up to $8 worth of food from the dollar menu. If I ordered Chinese food, I got an egg roll to go with every dish. I gained almost 20 pounds that February. Now I was depressed, confused, alone, failing school—and fat!

Gradually, I got disgusted by myself and tired of always being depressed. I was walking around in small T-shirts with a gut that hung low. My clothes felt tight. I felt like Homer Simpson with waves and a $5 tee.

I started wondering, "How am I going to get over my depression? What direction am I heading in life?" I wasn't the man I wanted to be. Getting high all the time was not helping me to be at peace. Finally, I couldn't stand myself anymore. I knew I had to change.

It helped when my ex and my mom called and reminded me of my good points. "You always had a presence when you entered a room," my ex told me. My mom said she thought of me as a determined guy who never let anyone stand in his way. I began to remember my good characteristics. I am a funny, determined, caring, real dude with a passion to write and a gift for making people smile.

I decided to test myself to see if I could stop smoking weed. I started slowly, going a day without smoking by keeping myself busy. I avoided the weed spots, went to school, the library and home.

My anger had always given me energy. Without it, I felt lifeless and exhausted.

I would get the urge to smoke at night. My anger had always given me energy. Without it, I felt lifeless and exhausted sometimes, as if the life force had drained out of me. I almost felt like if I didn't smoke or drink, I wouldn't wake up and feel alive.

But when I got the urge to drink, cry or smoke, I took long, 45 minute showers. It's a good thing my aunt didn't have to pay the water bill! I also started taking care of myself, putting on my jewelry, which I'd left on the dresser when I was depressed, and slowing down my eating to three meals a day.

I started a workout regimen—running up and down steps, doing push-ups and sit ups. I started to feel good physically. Seeing that I could take control of my life made my confidence grow. As I felt better, I started to keep busier and be more social. Each change made other changes happen. A year later, I'm still in the process of getting myself back.

Now I keep myself on the move—running in the morning, going to work in the afternoon. On weekends I chill with friends who don't smoke or drink, play basketball with my sister and take my little cousins to the movies. I don't have time to be alone and drink and smoke and reminisce about painful things.

The last time I smoked weed was four months ago. I was at my brother's apartment in Harlem. We ordered Chinese food, and one of my boys brought over an NBA game. We passed around some weed and drank orange juice and vodka while playing video games, and conversing about sports and music. I didn't turn down the weed, because it didn't seem like a big deal to smoke one time with friends.

But the next morning I felt physically sick. I was coughing hard and spitting non-stop. That turned me off to smoking. Since then I haven't smoked weed at all.

When I saw my brother again in November and he was smoking weed, I passed it up. When I turned it down, I felt powerful. I knew I could overcome my addiction to smoking weed. I was strict with myself and I stopped.

Since then, I've also cut down smoking cigarettes (to one or two a month) and I don't drink recklessly to deal with stress—just when I'm at a party or celebration.

Both my parents have bad lungs and livers and are perfect examples of what I don't want for myself. My father is sick and paralyzed on the left side of his face but he still smokes and drinks. Now I realize that my parents may have gotten addicted to smoking, using crack and drinking the same way I started: to cope with feelings of loneliness, anger and fear.

I can't say I won't have any more depressions, or that the urge to drink or smoke won't ever overtake me, because I don't know what life has in store, but I know I've made a big change. I feel more in control of myself than ever before.

Antwaun wrote this story when he was 19.
He later attended college and worked in retail.

Chris Pope

How Can You Mend a Broken Heart?

By Magda Czubak

"He doesn't like me."

That was the first thing I thought when I opened my eyes one Monday morning.

In the shower, my brain sent another unpleasant message: "He never liked me. He always liked Anna." (Anna was my ex-best friend.)

I left my house thinking, "Life stinks."

Why did my life stink? The answer is simple: a broken heart. For almost a year I had been desperately in love with my close friend, Mike, and I thought that having him love me back was the purpose of my existence. Then my friend Anna started to spend time with him, and he fell for her. (By the way, I was the smart one who introduced them to each other.)

I was very depressed. I was mad at Anna for starting to hang around with Mike in the first place. After all, she knew how much he meant to me. As for Mike—he was my first love and I was really hurt the feeling wasn't returned.

My self-esteem dropped as low as the temperature in Alaska. I spent whole days looking unsuccessfully for a meaning for my life. I was having pointless fights with my mom and I cried often, especially after Anna's calls about how happy she was with Mike. She thought I was over him, but the truth was I was hurt by them both.

The key to saying goodbye to my depression was getting involved in new interests and activities.

A year ago, I thought nothing in the world except Mike could help me feel better. I was wrong. I didn't realize that the world held many things that could heal my pain. To my surprise, the cure wasn't another guy to make me blush and sigh. I discovered that the key to saying goodbye to my depression was getting involved in new interests and activities.

Cure #1: Helping Others

The changes in my life began with a phone call from my friend, Martin, about a month after Anna and Mike got together. He asked me if I knew anyone who would like to tutor an 8-year-old girl from Poland, the same country I'm from.

"Yeah, me," I answered, only because I was looking for a way to earn money. The next day I met Kathy, my future student. She had been in the U.S. only a few weeks and needed somebody to teach her English. I agreed to come twice a week for two hours each time.

A week later, Martin found me two more customers, an 11-year-old boy and his 9-year-old sister. Spending 10 hours each week tutoring made me realize how rewarding it is to teach. When Kathy first started going to school here she couldn't understand anything. She felt lonely and sad. Now she loves school.

Being the one who helped her made me feel really good.

Tutoring gave me a feeling of independence and improved my self-esteem. Somebody was finally appreciating me. (All three children would sit waiting for me on their front steps, and jump up and down with enormous smiles when they saw me coming.) It also made me feel good that after being here only two years I could teach English to someone else. Furthermore, I enjoyed making my own money, and it was much more pleasant than sitting at home hopelessly wondering about that jerk going out with Anna.

Cure #2: Keeping Busy

Through school, I got involved in other activities that helped me get Mike off my mind. I got an internship at a kids' clothing company (internships are required at my high school) and also began volunteering at an animal shelter. Having a busy schedule helped my healing process. People at my internship helped me believe in myself because they appreciated my work, whether it was copying, filing, or proofreading.

My duties at the shelter—walking dogs, cleaning cats' cages, and feeding them—made me feel even more needed. I felt great and finally I was able to tell myself, "Life is not that bad." I didn't care anymore what "he" thought about me, or waste any more time wondering whether "he" would ever want to go out with me.

At least that's what I thought. Then, in the middle of February, Mike and Anna broke up, and he began calling me again. Any smart girl would have told Mike to get lost, but I wasn't that smart. I told him "yes" when he asked me out. I tried not to fall for him again, but soon I had big hearts in my eyes. They weren't as big and passionate as they had been the first time around (I was more careful) but I still had a lot of feelings for him, and then—after two weeks—he dumped me.

This time I was stronger than before. I cried myself to sleep that night and continued crying through the following day, but that's all. I told myself that if I could live without him two weeks ago, why not now?

After he disappeared from the pages of my diary this time, my life was fine. Not great, but just fine. Then, I asked my boss at my internship to hire me for the summer and he agreed. That changed it to great.

I was working 40 hours a week while most of my friends were having fun at the beach, but I didn't regret it at all. At work they trained me to do their billing. I entered invoices into the computer, printed them, and mailed them to customers.

I learned from my boss not to be afraid of a challenge, to always stay cool and face it. For instance, when I messed up with the paper at the printer, I just told myself, "It's OK, I can fix it." Later on, I applied this approach to the rest of my life. I realized that I could overcome all kinds of difficulties. My self-esteem grew a lot. I loved my job so much that I cried when they threw me a goodbye party at the end of summer. I've managed to keep working there part-time, three days a week after school.

I sometimes feel sad, but I always tell myself I can overcome it.

The other thing that made my summer great was that I did a lot of reading. I was looking for advice on finding someone special and keeping him, but the books helped me realize that I should not live for love and jump from the roof when I can't win somebody's affection.

I realized that love is only one part of life. The incident with Mike taught me not to fall so hard for a guy and not to wait for him to like me. Now I give a guy a few weeks and if he doesn't show any signs, too bad for him. I move on.

I'm a junior in high school now and I'm involved in a lot

of activities that make my life exciting. In addition to working part-time, I tutor, go to a gym and swim in the pool, read, study Spanish on my own, and of course go to school. I do all this during the week, so I have weekends free to see my friends. I feel I am more confident, independent, happy, and mature than I was a year ago.

Naturally I sometimes feel sad, but I always tell myself I can overcome it. I think about all the things I like to do and remind myself that every day of my life is important, and I shouldn't waste time by worrying. Doing things that I enjoy and setting goals and accomplishing them give my life meaning and make it fun.

Magda was 17 when she wrote this story. She later attended SUNY Binghamton, majoring in mathematics and computer science.

Stephanie "Meadow" Kunar

Starting Over Without Them

By Hattie Rice

When I was 13, I stopped going to school. The kids called me retarded and I had no friends. All I thought about was going home to play cards and watch TV with my mom. Being at home comforting my mom was a way to get away from the torment of school and to play my role in the family—daughter and psychiatrist to my mom.

I was afraid of leaving my mother alone. I worried that one day my problems (not liking people and stress, which were the problems she was aware of) and her problems (using drugs and hearing voices) would fall down on her and she'd die of stress.

I was 9 when my dad told me that he and my mom were schizophrenic. He was scared of people but could function. He was able to work. He said my mother had it worse. She heard voices and thought people were trying to drive her crazy and to kill her. To cope with the pain, she started smoking crack.

Soon her addiction started to show. She would steal money from the family. Sometimes we'd have no food in the house and would have to go to churches or beg at the welfare office. It made me feel embarrassed. I'd think, "This is not the way a kid should live, begging for food." I felt like she didn't care about me, because if she did, why would she spend our food money on crack?

Most of the time she was high and fidgety. When I touched her, she'd jump. Other times my mother would cry because of the voices and my dad would argue with her over her drug habit.

"You going to smoke up all the money," Dad would say.

"Please, just one more smoke," Mom would say.

My brother and I used to think, "Dad, why are you letting her do this to us?"

When I stopped going to school, a typical day with my mom started with her using half of the food money on crack and then coming home and smoking it. I'd usually check on her (because I could hear her talking to the voices) and she'd tell me to tell the voices to stop hurting her. I'd say a prayer for her and we'd play her favorite card game or watch television while I held her.

I wanted to be close to my mom, but I also felt like I needed to stay detached so her problems won't affect me the way they used to.

Then I'd give her my usual lecture, telling her the voices are in her head and that other people aren't doing it to her. I'd make clear that I didn't want to hurt her. I'd tell her she has a mental illness. My mom would hold me and cry when I comforted her.

It was hard feeling responsible for her, and sometimes it was overwhelming because I had my own problems. I also felt it wasn't a child's place to take care of her mother.

It was especially confusing to know that my mom was not in control of the way she acted. When she took our money to buy crack, I knew it was because she felt she needed it to cope with her problems, or when I tried to touch her or get close and she'd fidget, it was because of her addiction.

I'd tell myself not to be upset, because she wasn't trying to hurt me. But as much as I tried to understand, I also felt angry and abandoned. Even now I don't think I can ever forgive my mom for spending the food money. I think to myself, "If you really loved me, why would you do that to me? You saw how I was suffering."

Over time I got depressed. When I woke in the morning, I didn't want to leave the house because I felt like the world had nothing to offer me. At home I would cry. My frustration made me start eating a lot. I used to weigh more than 185 pounds.

My mother doing drugs had me feeling like life wasn't worth living. Eventually I figured I should just stay at home and avoid the world.

When I stopped going to school, I didn't think anybody would realize I was gone, but the attendance office called ACS, the child welfare agency in New York City. ACS sent a social worker to inspect our house, which was not in good shape. Every time the social worker came I stayed in my room. I think he recommended counseling for me because I would never talk to him.

The psychiatrist diagnosed me as having social phobia and I ended up being taken away from my family because they failed to make me go to school and didn't get my psychiatric prescription filled.

When I entered foster care, I was terrified. The first week, I stayed in my room and cried day and night. It was strange not to wake up and watch TV or play video games, and to have nobody to say "I love you" to. I just wanted to go back home.

Being in care felt scary because I knew my mom had nobody to console her. My parents came to visit every weekend. I felt better then because we'd go out for a walk and my mom would cry on my shoulder just like the old days.

But I soon began to feel relieved that the weight of my family's problems had been lifted off my shoulders. I realized that caring for my mom was hurting my life. I think my mom is able to get along without me. Unfortunately, that's because she smokes crack to forget about life. I feel upset about that, but it's become obvious to me that she needs more help than a child can give.

As I got settled into my placement, I realized I hadn't been getting all of the attention I needed at home. It felt good to focus on myself. There was not a lot of stress in the group home and if I needed someone to talk to there was always a staff on duty. I felt good knowing I had staff that led me in the right way and girls that helped lift my spirits. That's when I started to think that foster care is where I need to be.

In the group home, I can focus on my education and try to deal with my fear of people before it gets worse. I've started interacting with the girls well (and that's never been one of my specialties) and opening up about the anger I felt toward my mom by telling a new friend what I'd been going through at home.

During the first year of living without my parents, my depression lifted tremendously. As I talked more about my feelings and let them out, I didn't wake up crying like I did at home and I lost the weight I gained.

I started to realize that the world has many wonderful things to offer me, because I started to go outside, hang out with my friends and have fun. I was even able to go back to school and keep up an 85 average.

I realized that my depression was caused by stress at home and my failure to be able to communicate with people at school and make friends. Now I know that the only worries I need to have are about me, myself and I. It feels great to feel stronger and in control.

On my home visits, I saw that home was not where I needed to be because I saw my family still arguing over why there's no food money. Then they'd ask me for money. I'd be like, "I live in foster care and work a summer job. I ain't got no money."

I felt glad that I could go see them, but I also appreciated having the option to leave when things got too intense. I wanted to be close to my mom, to let her know I care for her and that she's not alone in this world, but I also felt like I needed to stay detached so her problems won't affect me the way they used to. Now when her problems become unbearable, it's back to my home away from home.

Not being surrounded by them has also me realize how mad I feel. I've always tried to cover up my feelings when I'm with my mom, because I figured that she has enough stress without knowing that she hurts me. But lately my feelings have been hurt so bad I can't cover them up, like when I think about how my mom and dad let us starve.

I need to let her know I'm angry at her and that everything between us isn't peaches and cream.

Then I blow up, screaming and yelling. My mom will say, "MoMo (that's my nickname), what did I do to upset you? Why do you act like this? I love you." Instead of telling her what's wrong I'll hold her and say, "Sorry, I love you."

I only outburst once in a while but it makes me feel calm and refreshed to let my feelings out and to stand up to my mom and give her what she deserves. It's frightening, too, because sometimes I feel like I might never stop.

Since I came into foster care, I've realized how much it affects me to keep a lot of stuff held in me that I need to release. Sometimes I feel confused because I wonder, "Is it OK to feel sympathetic and angry at the same time? And if I always release the sympathetic side, where is all my anger going? And if I don't want to hurt my mother, when or how will I release my rage?"

Any blind man can see that my parents want me home, because they ask me, "When are you coming home?"

and take me to my bedroom and ask me to spend a night. But whether they can actually care for me is the real question. (I think not, how about you?)

So after being in care for a year, I decided that going home would be a setback. In July, my social worker told my mom that I don't want to go home.

My mom asked, "Is that true?" I said, "Yes." She asked, "Why, MoMo? We love you." Before she could start acting like a baby, my social worker cut her off. That day, my social worker also had my mom take a drug test. Of course she tested positive, so my social worker might try to convince her to get help.

When I left I felt good, because I felt like my mom needed to be rejected. I need to let her know I'm angry at her and that everything between us isn't peaches and cream. I feel like I'm being selfish, but I have to help myself.

I do have doubts about putting myself first, though. I wonder, "Who is my mom going to have?" And it's scary to focus on myself. Before, whenever I was confused or frustrated about my own problems, I could focus on my mom instead. Now I have nobody else's problems to get me away from my reality.

I don't think my parents really understand my decision to stay in foster care. And I think my mom is confused when I say that she's mistreated me, because she really can't seem to see what she did wrong.

For so long I never showed the way I feel about her, so I think my mom still does not understand that her drug habit affects me. Maybe the only way she'll understand is if I tell her straight up or call the police on her when she smokes or buys crack.

Right now, I think it's better for me to wonder what she knows than to know for sure, because I don't want to find out the answer. Maybe I'll have the courage to find out someday.

Hattie was 15 when she wrote this story.
She attended college in New York.

Thaynia Waldron

Out of the Shadows

By Dina Spanbock

"Last night I was a four and now I'm a two," one kid said. I didn't know what he was talking about. As Steve, the program coordinator, called on other teens in the group, a dozen of them said similar things, adding on a goal for the day at the end.

Then Steve turned to me. "All right, Dina—now I'm going to ask you to introduce yourself, and tell us a little about why you're here," he said.

Now? Just like that? What was I supposed to say? That I was here because my dad died and I had stopped going to school and I needed to do something? And I had to say it to a room full of strangers?

I had struggled with depression and anxiety on and off for nearly five years. I only talked to a few of my close friends about it, but by sophomore year of high school, everyone at school could tell something was going on. Ever since my dad had died in the middle of freshman year, I'd been missing school a lot, sometimes for weeks at a time.

But if anyone asked where I'd been, I just said I hadn't been feeling well. After a while, they learned to stop asking. I avoided the subject at all costs. Sometimes, that was why I didn't go to school. I was ashamed and didn't want to have to explain to anyone that I was depressed. I was sure they would've been puzzled by the idea that living was so incredibly difficult.

But living was difficult for me. Depression makes everything difficult. It takes over your body, mind and spirit. Simple things like sitting up in the morning can take so much effort that by the time you do it, you're so tired that you need to lie back down.

By the middle of my junior year, I was sick of struggling every day, always having trouble getting to school. I decided something had to change. With the help of my psychiatrist, I decided to go to Four Winds, a psychiatric treatment center in Westchester that has programs specifically for adolescents. I wanted to be rid of my depression, or at least learn how to deal with it. I ended up learning a lot more than I expected.

I started commuting to Four Winds each day to take part in a three-month program. When I got there on the first day, I waited anxiously for my group therapy to begin. This was the morning check-in group, the staff told me, during which we were supposed to say how our night was and choose a goal for the day, anything from talking more in groups to not arguing with staff.

When they asked me to introduce myself, I spoke softly. "Um, I'm Dina. I'm here because I guess I've just been having, um, a lot of trouble, like, getting to school lately…"

Some of the other teens asked questions. I liked the easy ones.

"Where are you from?"

"Manhattan."

Then someone asked why I wasn't going to school.

"Well, my, uh, father died a couple years ago, and since then I, it's been, um, kind of hard for me to, um, go to school because of…depression," I said.

Steve explained that the numbers corresponded to feelings, one being great, five being in crisis. He asked me what I was at the moment. "Um, about a…a three?" I said, meaning that I was so-so. They moved on to the next person, and I became a bit closer to a 2.5.

We spent most of our time at Four Winds in various groups. Each group had a different aim, like discussing family conflict or medications. In the psychodrama group, we acted out situations and figured out how to respond. There was even a sharing group, where we had the opportunity to show other participants anything that we did or made, like art or photography. There was school for a couple of hours a day. And after lunch, we usually had a bit of downtime where we just hung around and talked.

I had a support system. The feeling of complete loneliness withered away.

As the days went by and the routines and people became more familiar, I became more comfortable there. I talked more about my feelings in group therapy. I began to give advice as well as take it. During sharing group, I sang. But I had to push myself to do all this. I still felt ashamed of being depressed and being at a treatment center.

One day, after a few weeks in the program, I woke up and my mood was pretty low. On the train to Four Winds, I only felt worse. By the time group therapy began, I was feeling suicidal.

I surprised myself by telling everyone at group that morning. I had sometimes told people about being suicidal once I felt better, but I had never told anyone I was suicidal while I still felt it. I was nervous that people would get really worried about me and just feel bad.

Other kids in the group started saying things like, "You're such a great person," and, "We would be so upset if you died," and, "Think about your family and friends." It was nice to hear I was wanted, but it didn't help much. I still felt terrible, and their words did not make me want to live.

Then a girl named Melanie spoke. "But when you're suicidal, you're selfish. You're not thinking about all the other people. You're so upset that nothing else matters. You can't worry about how other people would feel. You're too focused on how you're feeling."

I was in shock. All I could say was, "Yeah, exactly!" She knew what I was feeling even better than I did. She knew it and she could say it. I'd never really put what I felt into words before, but whatever I was feeling, I didn't think it was OK to feel that way.

You might not expect it in a place filled with depressed people, but we could laugh and smile and have a good time.

Melanie helped me realize what I was feeling: selfish. But not the kind of selfish you can help feeling, not the kind of selfish I should blame myself for feeling. Being suicidal meant all you could think about was how awful you felt, not about how it affected anyone else.

Melanie's words made me realize that it was OK to feel that way at times. Sure, it wasn't ideal to feel so down and I should work to change it if I could, but I realized I also shouldn't beat myself up inside for being depressed. It was just the way I felt. I couldn't help it; I didn't ask for it.

Her words also made me feel a connection. Not just with Melanie, but with everyone who had been through depression. I realized that we all shared something special that no one else could understand. It was almost like I was part of a worldwide club filled with strangers who I would instantly feel comfortable talking to.

I could talk about my trouble getting to school, or being

suicidal, or all the times I had hidden anxiety attacks in school. Talking to members of this "club" at Four Winds, hearing their experiences and relating mine to theirs allowed me to be happy for the first time in years. It helped me to get things off my chest, and my new friends' understanding responses helped even more. I had a support system. The feeling of complete loneliness withered away.

After that, when new people came to the program, I tried to make them comfortable. I showed them around, reassured them that this was a good place, asked them about their problems and often responded with my own story. I think it helped them, knowing they weren't alone.

We had fun, too. You might not expect it in a place filled with depressed people, but we could laugh and smile and have a good time. My friends Rob and Zoe and I used to go down to school every morning and afternoon together. But we didn't walk down the road from the main building to the school. We shuffled.

We shuffled our feet slowly but surely, all the while reminding each other and ourselves, "Shuffle!" It started out as a way to stall, but it became a way to make fun of ourselves. We joked about being mental patients, shuffling along the road rather than walking like "normal" people. Once a van drove by as we were shuffling along. "Ha ha, that van driver must know he's in a mental hospital now," Zoe laughed.

"Shuffle!" Rob shouted.

In unison, Zoe and I replied, "Shuffle!" And we continued, shuffling along to school.

In a way, our shuffling was the perfect metaphor for my entire experience at Four Winds. I took small steps, one at a time, and in the end, with others' help and support, I got to my destination. I learned to accept my depression.

I also learned ways to cope with my depression, like opening up and talking to people about my issues while they were going on, not just afterward. I learned breathing exercises to help with my anxiety. And I learned that in order to feel less depressed, I needed to stop isolating myself and get involved in activities even when I didn't feel like it.

Most of all, I was learning to feel comfortable in my own skin, comfortable with the fact that I was struggling, and even able to laugh and make fun of it. We all embraced our issues as a part of ourselves. In a way, I even began to be happy that I had struggled so hard, because it allowed me to go to Four Winds and meet these wonderful people I connected with so intensely. It was a connection that could only be made by fully understanding and talking about our hard times.

Leaving Four Winds after three months was extremely difficult. I loved my friends there. I didn't want to leave that world, where people understood and accepted my many issues, and where everyone could relate to me. But my program was finished and it was time to go.

One day soon after I left, I was sitting in the student lounge back at my old school, talking with some classmates. Somehow we had gotten onto the subject of medications people were on, I think because someone mentioned his attention deficit disorder.

"Ah, medication. So helpful," said Josh.

"I've been on everything," I said. "All my craziness will get you to at least try just about everything. I never used to think of depression as a mental illness, but that's what it is. I mean, clearly, with all these meds, I'm mentally ill," I said, smiling. I was so used to it being normal to talk like this among my Four Winds friends that I had forgotten other people don't see it this way.

No one said anything and an awkward silence filled the room. "And there goes my anxiety, skyrocketing," I thought as I sat uncomfortably in the silence.

But although it was awkward and I felt anxious, I'm glad I spoke about it. Hopefully, next time someone talks about mental illness with my classmates, particularly depression, they won't feel quite as uncomfortable.

Depression isn't a subject people talk about openly very often. When they do, it's usually very serious. But that's not how I talk about it now. I'm no longer ashamed of my struggles and I don't want to go back to feeling that way. If it comes up, I tell my story, no matter who's there. I let people know that there's nothing to hide or be ashamed of. I do this in the hope that some day, depression will become less taboo.

I know depression doesn't just go away. It continues to be a struggle for me and probably will be for quite some time. Luckily, I have the support of my friends from Four Winds who I've stayed in touch with. And although I'm still learning how to cope with my depression, I've taken the most important step—I've accepted that it's a part of me.

Dina was 19 when she wrote this story.

Dani Reyes Mozeson

Brotherly Love

By Jessica Vicuña

My mom was always working and my dad was...well, he simply wasn't around. Growing up, it seemed like my oldest brother Adolfo was the only one who made time for me.

Even when I was little, Adolfo always talked to me and took me places. We'd hang out in parks and watch movies together. He'd play stupid Ken and Barbie with me. When I was 8 and he was 21, he started taking me along to his college classes. I remember staring at him as he wrote down a bunch of squiggly lines and thinking to myself, "My brother is a genius." (I later learned that he was taking music theory and those squiggly lines were musical notes, not Egyptian hieroglyphics.)

But the coolest thing about my brother was simply the way he treated me—like I was an adult, even though I was only in the 3rd grade.

My childhood Christmases were the best times because Adolfo made them memorable. He gave me cool dolls instead of corny stuffed animals.

When blizzards hit, Adolfo would carry me downstairs kicking and screaming because I knew he would throw me into the deepest snow mound on the block and leave me there. When I finally dug myself out of the snow, frostbite and all, I would try to run upstairs to regain my warmth. Before I could reach the door, someone would catch me in a bear lock. Yes, you guessed it—Adolfo. He would be hiding behind the door downstairs, waiting for a chance to throw me back into the snow. I think he liked torturing me, but I didn't mind. It was fun.

The fun lasted until I was 13. That's when all the child stuff was suddenly over and everything happened to me with a big bang. Things like menstruation, low self- esteem, idiot boys, and just questions, questions, questions about life.

Instead of talking to Adolfo about the changes I was going through, I tried hard not to show them to him. I didn't want him to know—I was too embarrassed.

I was also afraid. You see, my brother is very old-fashioned. He believes that women should act a certain way and young ladies should behave in a proper manner. If I ever told him that I liked a boy in class, forget it, he'd flip out. And if I tried to disagree with him, it would be a waste of time because he was always right.

I was afraid that if I told him the truth about what was going on with me, he would either preach or criticize or just make me feel stupid. It was easier for me to be the kind of sister who had a smile and good grades. I felt that my brother had me on this "good little sister" pedestal. I was scared that he would stop treating me like I was special when it was finally brought to his attention that I wasn't a cute little girl anymore, just a confused teenager. Part of me wanted to sit down with him and pour out my entire heart, but I couldn't do it.

Things got a little better when I started high school. Junior high had been hell because all the popular kids hated my guts. I had feared high school would be the same, but it wasn't. I wound up meeting a lot of cool, interesting friends, schoolwork was easy, and life was good—for the first few months, anyway.

It didn't last. By the third quarter of ninth grade, I was totally unsatisfied with myself. Schoolwork seemed to get harder and harder. Each test I took felt like it was written in another language because I couldn't understand the questions. I was so discouraged I didn't even show up for half of my classes. Pretty soon, I was running an F average. I got angry with myself and felt even more stupid because I was flunking.

It was easier for me to be the kind of sister who had a smile and good grades.

I was depressed beyond the definition of the word. I was failing school and didn't understand what was going on inside of me. How could I have let it get this far? I was out of control for reasons that I couldn't define.

I wanted to tell Adolfo—about the flunking, about the depression, about me and him, everything. But I didn't.

I hardly spoke to anyone in the house, and my moodiness was overbearing. My family knew something was up, but no one cared to find out what the problem was—except Adolfo. He noticed my change of attitude and confronted me about it several times. When he asked what was wrong, I would tell him, "Nothing," and change the subject.

By the beginning of 10th grade, my attitude was starting to bother him. So when I went away on a school trip for a weekend in mid-October, Adolfo decided to call up my school and find out what was up.

All through the trip I felt nervous, but I didn't know why. I guess it was a liar's intuition or something. When I got home that Sunday afternoon, my brother was waiting for me, all disappointed. I knew it was about my grades. I just knew he knew.

"You know," Adolfo started saying, "I called up your school Friday morning."

"Ah-huhh?" I said, thinking, "Dead meat!"

"I was talking to someone who was your seminar teacher," he said in a nonchalant tone.

"Oh yeah, Leo, he's my teaching seminar teacher..." I was so freaking nervous.

"Fs? He said you've got all Fs!"

"I know, life sucks!" I immediately told him.

"Why didn't you tell me what was going on?" Adolfo asked calmly.

At this point I was ready to break the dam, let all that water that had been building up inside me break loose. I was just scared that all that water might start a flood, and I think Adolfo was scared too. I wasn't sure if he was ready for this.

"Well, Adolfo, it's like this..." It came out. The dam broke. I told him everything. About the depression and not being sure why I had it in the first place, about school and not knowing why I couldn't concentrate on my studies, and about every burning, nauseating feeling I had in the pit of my heart.

My brother Adolfo was sad. Every time I cry, it gets to him. His eyes get sad and his voice drops to a deeper range. At that moment, he saw the real me. The me nobody knew.

As Adolfo started to comfort me with words of encouragement and understanding, I started to see snippets of Kodak color memories. Like when he would pick me up and fly me around like a baby jet airplane. Or the time he put on this big scary hideous monster mask and chased my sister and me around the house like a madman.

I felt like I'd lost the little girl inside of me forever. And when my brother sat there and tried to console me like a therapist, I felt he knew I'd lost that little girl too. He sat there, across from me on the bed, just looking at me. No hugs, no kisses, just analytical talk.

This was the moment that I had been afraid of. But it wasn't what I had expected. There wasn't any criticism, no angry vertical vein line on his forehead, no preaching on how improper it was to keep things from him, nothing. He wasn't looking at me through the eyes of a big brother. He was looking at me through the eyes of an adult.

The funny thing about it was that I felt some form of respect from Adolfo. He was ready to move our relationship into a different realm. This conversation was the beginning of something really mature for us. I wasn't his little kid sister anymore, and we both knew it. And it was OK.

At that moment, he saw the real me. The me nobody knew.

It's been more than two years since that moment, and a lot has changed. For one thing, I'm not screwing up in school any longer. I changed schools and I actually like it now. Another is that my relationship with my brother is stronger then ever because of that talk we had. I've gotten to know who he really is and to see him as a human being rather than the "giant holy brother" that I had made him out to be.

I don't feel stupid telling him about my feelings anymore. I can open up to him without being put on the spot. I'm not trying to be a good little sister anymore. When I make a mistake, I admit it and tell him. I decided that if he gets upset, then he gets upset, but so far he hasn't. He even took it pretty well when I started going out with this guy...until the lad broke my heart. Then my brother saw red. I guess the overprotective side of the feelings he has for me hasn't been put to rest completely.

My fear that my brother wouldn't like the grown-up me has gone and left without a trace. Now that I look back, I realize that everything would've been easier if I'd told him about my emotions sooner. Then maybe the whole flunking and depression fiasco wouldn't ever have happened.

But I'm actually glad that it did happen. Good things came

out of what seemed like a period of hell. I've gotten to like myself more. I'm not afraid to make mistakes any more because I understand that I can learn from them. And I no longer run away from my mistakes. I confront them.

This change couldn't have happened without my brother's help. I want to thank you, Adolfo, for being there for me when no one else was. For being the best brother that any sister could ever have.

Jessica was 18 when she wrote this story.
She attended the School of Visual Arts and started a
successful business.

Gamal Jones

Dealing With Death

By Griffin Kinard

I was born on a hot summer day, not knowing what the individual upstairs had in store for me. My family was two million miles short of perfect. My father was hitting and abusing my siblings and me for no reason. My mother left as soon as she could.

Then the Administration for Children's Services came and separated me from my family, seemingly without a care. A van would take us to court. After court we would all pack up the van again, only to see each other get off at different locations.

The pain that I felt from watching first my mother, then my father, then my brothers leave me was unforgettable. I felt betrayed by my own people. It just killed me to see my family torn away one by one.

After a few foster homes and a hospital I was placed at a residential treatment center, where I stayed for the next nine years.

Nothing but pure hell, really. That's all I can say.

I thought the abuse and the separations were enough mental testing for one person. Then the people close to me started leaving me for good.

When I was 9, my father went from being a man of strength to a man who needed to be pushed around in a wheelchair. He died of AIDS.

After my father died, I became reckless. I acted like nothing mattered. Looking back, I see now that I was rushing my own death. I could not bear the thought of being alive. I started to go off on my own all the time. I was so sad that I was nobody's friend, and that my family did nothing but mess with me.

> *Looking back, I see now that I was rushing my own death. I could not bear the thought of being alive.*

Eventually, I thought that killing myself was the answer. I tried to kill myself over and over again, but I failed each and every time. I think that part of me wanted to live. I wasn't crazy. I was just too small to have experienced all that abuse, my mother disappearing and my father dying.

It took me years of spazzing out to move on. Finally, I did. I calmed down a lot. But the fight wasn't over yet.

In the summer of 2003, when I was 16, I was in class when my social worker came and got me and took me to her office. She told me, "Griffin, your brother was shot." I was not shocked to hear the news because my brother had been shot before.

So I replied, "OK, is he in the hospital? Can I see him?"

"No, Griffin. Your brother was shot three times in the head."

The feelings that came over me I cannot explain. My social worker asked me if I was all right.

"Yeah, I'm fine," I told her. Then I walked out of her office, only to see a door with a glass window. I punched the glass, but was still not fine. I could not get what she said out of my head.

I could not grasp the truth. I repeated to myself, "My brother is not dead."

I arrived outside with tears in my eyes and blood dripping from my right hand. I started walking my way toward the busy street (not knowing why) but a voice in my head stopped me. It reminded me that people looked up to me.

That made me stop and think about a few things. Like, why is it that I cause harm to myself every time something devastating happens to me? Who in the hell was that talking inside my head? And why in the heavens am I walking toward a busy street?

After all that passed I was on the road to bury my brother. The funeral was set right on my birthday. I was not thrilled by this, but there was nothing I could do.

The last time I saw my brother he was cold like an iceberg. I was convinced my brother no longer had a soul. I felt nothing but pure sadness and anger. I did not see the point of living anymore.

It is very hard to find light when life gives you nothing but chaos and devastating situations.

That night after burying my brother, I thought to myself, "I am a knight and so was my brother. A knight is someone who plays the game down to the last dollar. He doesn't give up. Once he's in, he's in."

People always told me that I was a bright kid and that I could go far. I didn't believe their words at the time. But remembering my brother in his coffin, I really understood that life was short and I needed to make the most of mine.

Soon I was moved to Brooklyn House, a place where too many things happened. But the good part was I got a mentor who came to see me damn near every weekend.

We were real cool. He was white, I was black. It looked like opposites do attract. We went to the movies every weekend. Holidays we spent as his place. It was awesome. You could not tell me nothing, nothing at all. I was having fun. I was enjoying it, but it was like all good things—they come to an end.

It was two weeks before Thanksgiving that I last saw Dale. We were planning what to do for the holiday. Basically, the same thing that we always did: go to his place and chill.

About a week later I walked into the group home and sat down to watch some television when the supervisor called me down to his office. He told me that my mentor had passed.

I was stuck on stupid, again. I didn't know what to do or say. I just cried tears of confusion. I thought, "Just a week ago we were making plans for Thanksgiving, and his family is making plans to bury him now?"

It is very hard to find light when life gives you nothing but chaos and devastating situations. Losing my mentor and my family has not been easy to handle. I wanted to break down, give up. I had feelings I could no longer explain. I did not express my feelings to anybody. I felt like they were too raw to express.

To get through it I had to dig deep into my soul. When I got some time alone I was able to sit back and look at my life. I wrote a poem called "DLS." It was about someone dying and speaking their last words to their loved one, telling them that they love them no matter what.

Finding out that I could put my emotions on paper gave me the cockiest feeling in the world. I felt tough and ready for what the world threw at me. Soon I learned how to channel my feelings into poetry to the point that now the pen and the pad are my two best friends.

To this very day, I still use poetry to express myself. For damn near every situation I go through, I write a poem. Writing all that sadness and painful madness down has made those feelings just part of my past.

Now I remind myself, "Death is just death, not something to tear you apart. It's what we all wish for—peace and quiet." My time will come, but for now I try to enjoy everything life throws at me and to stay focused on the long run. Destiny is like a sloppy hill, a lot of ups and downs.

Going through all of this could drive any man or woman crazy, but I remind myself that the ups will come again. I've got to keep a clear head in the darkness and search out the light. I've got to keep my motivation, my determination.

I tell myself, "Keep your mother-loving head up. Be proud of your past, accept your present, and embrace your future." I can keep the ones I lost in mind, but I must move on with my life.

Griffin was 20 when he wrote this story.

How to Cope With Life's Losses

By Shameeka Dowling

Every teen has faced a loss of some kind. I wanted to know how teens can cope with loss, so I interviewed Demy Kamboukos, Ph.D., a clinical psychologist and director of research for the Families Forward Program in the Institute for Trauma and Resilience at the New York University Child Study Center.

Q: How would you define loss?

A: Loss can be the death of a loved one, a close family member or a friend. There are also losses due to social circumstances—if parents divorce, there's the loss of daily contact with a parent who moves out. Teens can also experience a loss of resources, such as a change in finances, and loss of friendships and close family relationships, either because of arguments or because someone moves away.

Q: How do teenagers typically react to death?

A: Teenagers have similar reactions to adults—sadness, depression, disbelief, potentially anger. Teenagers also start to really question their own mortality: "Who am I, what's my purpose in life, what am I going to do to make a difference?" A death might change a teenager's goals, their sense of obligation to others and their sense of self.

Q: What is the best way for a teen to deal with the recent loss of a family member?

A: The first thing teenagers should understand is that it's normal to feel sad, but it's also normal to feel angry or confused. It's also normal to want to continue doing what you planned to do with your life, even though you've lost a loved one.

Sometimes what happens when someone dies is that no one talks about them and no one knows how to react. And then teenagers are not given the opportunity to share memories about the person they love and miss.

It's important to talk about your feelings, to share your memories and thoughts about the person who died.

It's also important to maintain routines. Finding positive experiences and participating in after-school activities helps with recovery. It's OK to do that, even though you're sad, even though you're missing someone you love dearly. Also, teenagers who give back to their community and who volunteer tend to do well because it gives them a sense of purpose, serves as a distraction, and makes them feel good helping others in need.

Q: What are some ways a teenager can handle the loss of a certain environment, such as the house they grew up in or the country they come from?

A: Loss related to social or environmental factors may not have the same effects as the loss of a loved family member. However, that's not to minimize how important the effect of such loss may be. For example, if you can't go back to your country or if you have to move away from the house you grew up in, you may lose a sense of who you are, your social support and your daily routines.

Teenagers should seek people around them who they can talk to about their feelings, build strong new relationships, and find ways to build on positives in their new environment. I would recommend joining an after-school group or team and finding ways to give back to the community.

Q: Where can teenagers find programs or help to deal with their losses?

A: Our website, AboutOurKids.org, has a lot of resources for families and teenagers. If you feel down or sad most of the time, are not able to concentrate, don't want to do things you used to think were fun, or are unable to continue with daily activities, these are some indications you may need some help.

I would say first, if you can, speak to an adult you trust, such as a parent, teacher, guidance counselor or doctor. They can help you look into resources in your community. It may be helpful to speak with a professional about your feelings.

Q: How can teens help friends dealing with loss?

A: It's really hard for teenagers when their friends are going through loss. Sometimes the inclination is to pretend it didn't happen, or to try to fix it and make it all go away. It's normal to have those feelings. But it's important to be a good listener and a support to your friend.

Tell them, "I'm here for you; whenever you want to talk, I'm ready to listen." Teens also need to understand that sometimes someone's not ready to talk and share their feelings, and that's OK. Teens can also help their friends by getting them involved in everyday activities and events.

---

*Shameeka was 17 when she conducted this interview.
She graduated high school and went to SUNY Purchase.*

Amaury Almonte

Worn Down

By Anonymous

After Christmas vacation last year, I stopped going to school. Every morning I would wake up to go to school and feel nauseous. The nauseous feeling made me too sick to take the hour train ride to school. I thought it was because I never got enough sleep or because I wasn't eating well.

At first, my mom kept waking me up for school every morning. She would yell at me that I was throwing away my life. For a while I'd been going to school off and on. But after a straight week of me not going, my mother stopped trying to wake me up. She gave up on me.

I knew she was disappointed in me, and everyone else in my family expressed their disapproval. What hurt the most was that my brothers called me a high school dropout.

Every time my younger brother said I was a dropout, I wanted to smack him in the head and yell, but I never did that. I just felt like more of a failure and more anxious to become a success.

I've always felt like my family has high hopes for me—they want me to be the first person in my mother's family to go to college. But I also think that they don't believe I will do well. They seem as unsure as I am that I can succeed.

I want to prove those doubts wrong. I especially want to prove to myself that I can finish high school and go to college. But last year I felt like I couldn't handle school.

At the end of January, I started getting really bad chest pains. I'd had those pains before, and they would just come and go. But the one I had in January was agony, like a vampire had driven a stake through my heart. After that episode, I told my mother.

My mom took me to the doctor, who poked around my chest and asked me questions like, "Have you been going to school? How many brothers or sisters do you have? Where are your mom and dad?"

In the end she told me that I might be depressed, and that the nausea and chest pains could be symptoms of stress. She said she knew a good social worker that I should talk to. She made an appointment for me to see him.

Feeling depressed explained a lot of the stuff that had been happening, like that I was feeling lazy and sad and sleeping too much. It made sense to me when the doctor explained depression. Since my mother didn't know how I was feeling, I'm not sure she understood, but she always made sure that I went to my appointments.

The first time I went to the social worker I was scared. I was afraid that he might think I was crazy or that he was just a nosy busybody. I was uncomfortable the first four sessions, but the more I talked to him, the more I revealed secrets I never knew I had.

It made me feel better having someone to talk to who didn't know my family and didn't already have an opinion about which side to be on. Every time I talked to him I felt happier, like a five-ton weight had just lifted off my shoulders.

Mostly, I talked to my therapist about my responsibilities at home and my relationship with my father. I think a lot of my depression revolves around my father's abandonment of my family when I was 7.

My mother always told me my father went to China to earn some money. It was supposed to be temporary, but he never came back to live with us.

For a long time after he left, my father would come back every couple of years. He would stay only a day or two, because his most important reason to be in the U.S. was business with his clients.

In my family, we never talk about him except when he calls. I don't know much about his relationship with my mom because he left when I was little, but from what my mother told me, he didn't treat her well.

With him not around, my mom has had to really struggle to support our family. She usually works 13 hours a day, seven days a week, in her parents' Chinese restaurant.

We live in a small apartment above the restaurant that is too crowded. Nine people live in three tiny bedrooms, and until this year, I shared a room with my mom and my two little brothers.

I'm the oldest and the only girl, so I have to help my mom. A lot of responsibilities and expectations fall on me.

For years, I had to work almost every day after school and all weekend in the restaurant. I also have to translate for my entire family and read their mail.

Because I speak English, they drag me from one place to another—like to the DMV, citizenship tests, school officials, the health department, and doctors. Sometimes I feel so irritated that I want to grab one of the letters and throw it on the floor and stomp on it. I never do that, though, because they would probably think I went crazy. Plus, it's disrespectful.

At the same time, I have to go to school and I'm expected to do well there. It might not seem a lot to some, but it's a lot to me.

I always thought that if my father was around, I would be much happier. He would help support us, my mother would not have to work so much, and I would not have to help her work. I always wanted to do after-school activities or hang out with friends, but I never have the time.

If he was still here supporting us, all my brothers and I would have to do is concentrate on school and have a normal childhood.

We would probably live in our own house, I wouldn't have stopped going to school, and I would be in my first year in college. But instead, we have to take his place and be the father while we're still kids.

My memories of my father aren't all so bad. I used to be his little girl, his favorite. I would cry for him when I had a nightmare or when my family would tease me about being fat. He used to yell at my mother when she would yell at me.

When I was younger, everything seemed normal about my family. My memories seem like a fairy tale. As I got older, I started to understand that my family was dysfunctional.

I was a kid, and kids are not supposed to know about secrets in the family.

When I was in sixth grade, my mother was crying all the time and my grandparents were yelling at my father. I didn't understand why, until I found out that he was cheating on my mom and that he had another daughter by that woman. He even gave that daughter my Chinese name. That hurt me so much.

At first I wasn't sure it was true. And I couldn't ask. I was a kid, and kids are not supposed to know about secrets in the family. But I became positive of his cheating when I visited him in China that summer and saw his baby girl. That's when I lost respect for my father.

When I was little, my father would sometimes ask me how I would like having another mom. My mom used to blush and laugh when he asked that. We thought he was teasing. Now I wonder if he was already cheating on my mom back then.

S till, I always felt that some day he might come back to us again. Then, two years ago, my father came back because he wanted to get his marriage certificate. The United States government was about to take away his American passport since he had been living in China for such a long time.

My mom didn't want to give him the certificate. She thought that if he didn't have a passport, he would stay with us in the United States. So she went into hiding because she knew my father would badger her until she gave in.

He came at night and waited for my mother until the morning.

"Damn woman," I heard him mutter to himself. "Morning and she's still not home."

He started to shake me awake. "Where your mother went?"

"I don't know," I said, my heart beating so fast. I cursed at him silently, thinking, "Damn him! Why did he have to come?"

He started cursing and went to wake up my brother.

"She's at little aunt's house," my brother said. "Go away, I want to go back to sleep."

I was shocked. "Traitorous brother telling him where our mother is. I am going to smack him later," I reminded myself.

My father came in the room again.

"Where is your aunt's house?"

"I don't know." I was beginning to sound like a parrot.

He looked at me like he wanted to smack me. He knew I was lying but I didn't care. Then he began ranting and raving like a little boy whose candy was stolen from him. I pushed myself against the wall to get as far away as I could. I was afraid he might hit me. But instead he looked at my brand new computer with a crazed look.

"If you don't tell me, I am going to grab the computer and smash it on the floor," he threatened. I started crying. I never cry, but I couldn't take the stress of having to handle this situation all by myself. I thought, "Why did Mommy leave me to deal with this?"

"I am going get some guys," he threatened, "and have them beat up your aunt's family."

I was afraid that he would actually do that and I didn't want my family hurt. So I told him that I would call her house. In the end, my dad got the papers. My mom didn't say anything, and we didn't talk about it.

And I never told my family what he said. I didn't want people to know that my father is the kind of person who would have his own family beaten up. After that, I didn't want to see him anymore.

Some might say that I have to love him because he is my dad. But I don't. He stopped being my father when he left. I might sound bitter and angry, and I am. He is the father, not me. I want to be a child.

Part of me does sometimes wish that he would come back to help, or at least send money, but I

The more I talked to him, the more I revealed secrets I never knew I had.

don't want him disrupting our lives. Usually, after I've seen him or talked to him, I just feel worse. He only calls when he needs something.

Everything with my father makes me feel angry, betrayed, and confused.

Though he doesn't know how I feel, I want him to know. I don't like having him think that he is welcome back in the family any time. I don't like my mom having him think this way, either. I want to be able to scream and yell at him, but I never have the courage to.

All this anger at my father, combined with the stress of my family responsibilities, made me feel very depressed. I really wanted to escape from everything. Around the time I left school, whenever I felt down, I would think, "Why can't I just die right now?" At times, when I was feeling really sad, I'd think about getting a long piece of rope and hanging myself.

When that thought was racing through my head, I was scared. I was never close to killing myself, because every time I had a weak moment, the thought of someday becoming a success kept me strong.

If I killed myself, I would never be able to prove that I am not a failure, like I sometimes feel I am. I would never be able to make my father regret leaving us.

I guess I started thinking about suicide so much because I felt like I just couldn't take it anymore. I wanted to be able to get as far away as I could from everything that was making me feel so angry and stressed.

F inally, I told my mom that I couldn't work in the restaurant anymore. She said we couldn't afford for me to stop completely, so now I only work on Saturdays. I have more free time to get away from my house, to do my homework, and to see friends.

When I started high school, I never hung out with any friends after school. I felt really lonely. So this is a big change.

Other times, I just walk around from store to store window shopping, or I go to the library and read. I feel so free going out and doing whatever I want and knowing that no one can contact me if they want something done.

I know I feel better than before. Last fall, I went to a new school. Now I do things I never could have imagined doing, like intern at different companies for school credit and talk to complete strangers.

Going to the counselor has helped me figure out what's bothering me and let some of those feelings go.

I'm not completely over my depression, though. Lately, my mood has been going up and down. One moment I will be laughing with my brothers and the next I will be throwing things at them.

The littlest thing that happens at home can cause me so much anxiety. The other day, my brothers were coming in and out of my room to ask me stupid questions. I was feeling irritated with them, but I didn't want to yell at them because that might end up as a fight.

But finally I had to scream at someone. That someone was my mother. She called and started bothering me and I exploded. I started yelling at her to leave me alone.

I hate yelling at people I care about, but when I get stressed I just can't seem to help it. I get bottled up so tightly, I snap at anyone in my way.

Sometimes I feel like hiding under my blankets. Other times I feel like embracing every event that is going on.

What I really want now is to finish high school so I can go to a far away college and get away from home. It makes me happy that I have actually gotten accepted to a college. It's not the best college in the world, but it's a start.

I want to become successful, or at least graduate from college, so I can prove to my family that I can make it. I still feel unsure about myself, though. Sometimes I worry that I'm not smart enough to get good grades or that I will screw up like I did during high school.

I want to say that I have complete confidence in myself that I will be OK, but I can't. I don't know that I won't mess up in college.

I want to be able to tell my father that I have become a successful person and that he had nothing to do with it. And it's important to me for my mother to be able to say, "My daughter is in school and she's studying to be a doctor or a computer expert." I want everyone to look at me and think that my mother did a wonderful job.

The writer was 18 when she wrote this story. She later attended SUNY Albany, where she majored in economics.

The World in My Head

By Natasha Santos

"Tasha, what did he do to you?" my aunt asks me in the middle
of the night. This is the second night in a row that she has roused
me from my sleep. Her eyes are bloodshot and downcast. She's
tired and guilty.

"I don't know," I tell her with big wide eyes and whispers. I
know what she's talking about, but I've been sworn to secrecy.
My uncle has made me promise that I wouldn't tell a soul about
what we've been doing. "Promises are supposed to be kept," he'd
told me.

"Do you want a sip?" My aunt offers me some of the beer
she's been cradling. I take a sip—it's sour and too cold. I don't
like it. "Now, what did he do to you?" she repeats. I guess she
feels the drink has loosened me up. It hasn't—I'm frustrated and
ashamed and scared that Uncle Tony will find out I told and be

mad.

"I don't know," I say, as I start crying. And I didn't know. There were no words in my vocabulary to explain the way his fingers have been exploring my body for the past several weeks. I don't know how to explain the way my body responds and how I could never help that I was often alone with him. I don't know how to make her understand that it wasn't really all my fault and that I'm sorry and that I will never do it again. She surely won't listen if I tell her what's been going on.

She eventually gives up and sends me to bed. She goes back into the bedroom that she shares with Uncle Tony and I hear the bed squeaking a few minutes later.

I stay up listening to their sounds and thinking my thoughts. I can't sleep because my head is too full of thoughts and feelings that I can't express. There's no one around to talk to and, if there were, no one that I would trust to hold some of these feelings. So I just lie there and let my imagination take over and take me out of myself. I imagine that I'm a beautiful princess and that I have to save myself from the evil witch who wants to kill me so that she can become royalty.

I imagine that I have to run away from the witch and go on this long journey to my parents, who will protect me with their magical powers. I just have to follow the yellow brick road (I had just read *The Wizard of Oz*) and dodge the witch and her evil helpers. I use my wits and my powers to outsmart the witch every time.

The world that I imagine is so intricate and busy and scary and happy and wonderful that I forget that I'm on the couch in the living room with my aunt and uncle and their sounds.

I first noticed my habit of transporting myself to other worlds in my mind that night at my aunt's house. I felt special and smart that I could create these worlds in my head.

When I was younger it was all about the TV shows I watched and books I read. They were fuel for my imagination. I would pretend that I was one of the characters in the TV show and live in their worlds even after the half hour was over. Fighting the bad guys, saving the day, and still making it home in time to be tucked into bed by my loving parents. I wanted those things, but they didn't exist for me anywhere but in my mind.

I couldn't control my mother's behavior or my father's absence, but I could control my mind. My characters and fantasies existed as a safe haven. This was my escape from my mother's neglect, my uncle's hands, and my teacher's looks of apathy or disgust. In my imagination I was strong and wise and loved by all. No one could challenge me and no one could make me less than I was with looks or disregard or slaps in the face. It was perfect.

I can't sleep because my head is too full of thoughts and feelings that I can't express.

Later it became my escape from my foster mother, Diane. When you were being punished for some small infraction of her rules (this happened often—I was once put on punishment for a month because I forgot to brush my teeth), you would have to spend the day (or days) standing in the hallway.

Her kids, who were never on punishment, would often walk by and make snide comments that you couldn't answer back to because you weren't allowed to talk. There wasn't much to do but stand there, think, and figure out a way to deal with the situation. Standing there for hours on end really got me into the habit of using my mind to escape.

As I grew older I became more and more conscious of my imagination. By the 7th grade I had moved out of Diane's house and into another foster home where I was alone most of the time. My foster family was never there, and I didn't mesh well with the kids in my new school, so I didn't have any friends.

I was using my imagination constantly as a source of entertainment and comfort. While the other kids were being mean to me and my family was being…my family, I went inside myself to get out of it.

Soon, though, people in school started to say that I mumbled to myself and that I was crazy. My mother started asking me if I saw people or heard voices. Up until that point I had thought that what I did was normal, that everyone did it and no one minded. I was wrong in a big way.

Soon psychiatrists were asking me if I heard voices or saw people, and the kids in school found more ammo to shoot at me. My mind was betraying me big time but I wasn't ready to part with my imaginary worlds. So I didn't stop, just toned it down. I made myself more aware of other people and tried not to mumble to myself in public.

I've been thinking about it all lately, probably because I've just turned 18 and am trying out this new phase in my life while still making sense of my childhood. I have all these thoughts and questions about what I need to be a successful adult, or at least one that doesn't end up on welfare with 20 kids and a drug habit.

I am worried that this habit of escaping reality could lead to bigger problems. Now I escape with my imagination, but what will I do when 10 years of adulthood have jaded my imagination and creativity and I begin looking for other ways of dealing? Will I turn to drugs? Will my imagination turn off and my mind turn to depression?

A lot of the adults I know are too bored with their lives and work to do anything creative or use their imaginations for something other than balancing a checkbook. Then there are those adults you see on the train talking to themselves and making everyone around them uncomfortable. I don't want to run from myself, and I don't want people to think I'm crazy and run away from me. I want people to want to be around me. I want to be able to stay around my real self.

I brought this up one day with Rachel, my therapist, because I was wondering how destructive my habit really was. We have weekly sessions where we talk about anything under the sun. Well, anything I want to, anyway.

Rachel was surprisingly supportive of my imagination get-aways. I told her about how I developed my habit of mentally escaping and that I wanted to stop it. I didn't tell her about the "thinking aloud," though, or my fear of not being able to handle reality when I'm older.

"Well, from what you're telling me, I think that this habit you have is positive and I don't think that you need to be too concerned about giving it up—from what you're telling me." It was clear that she knew there was more to the story. But I wasn't ready to tell her everything yet. I don't agree that I can keep this habit up the way I've been doing it. In the future, I'll have to find some other way of coping that I haven't figured out yet.

> *I couldn't control my mother's behavior or my father's absence, but I could control my mind.*

After we talked, I looked back at the times when I was too young and too powerless. I never want to be so young and powerless again that I need to go inside of myself to hide from reality. I want to be strong and confident enough to face things myself.

I'm still worried that if I don't give up the pretend world in my head then I will never become a productive adult, one who can take care of herself and live life on her own terms. And I think that my mind has also gotten tired of creating alternate realities for itself.

In the past, when I had a bad memory or an ugly thought, I wouldn't allow myself to feel it or take the time to understand what had happened to me. I just looked through my mental Rolodex and found something else to think about. But that is not completely OK with me anymore. Sometimes I can get so lost in my mind that I forget where I am. I make sporadic movements and mumble to myself, like that crazy person on the train.

I hope there is a way for me to deal with some of my past

memories without only using my mind haven. Somebody suggested writing out my experiences, or talking about them. I'm not ready to speak about a lot of things. But when I am, I hope I can find someone receptive and open to hear me.

Natasha was 18 when she wrote this story.
She attended the University of New Orleans.

Phillip Rollano

Dealing With It

By Hazel Tesoro

Fifteen and a half hours into the 18th year of my life, and dark circles twitched beneath my eyes. A woman whom I hated passionately—the regional supervisor of the group home in San Francisco where I had been living for 18 months—handed me the first piece of chocolate cake. Then the program director recounted a memory of me, while a room filled with people I wanted to forget like a bad dream laughed.

Afterwards, Mr. Head Honcho himself handed me a $100 check and a graduation certificate with a quote from Benjamin Franklin: "The Constitution only guarantees the American people the right to pursue happiness. You have to catch it yourself."

The going-away party had already consumed 10 minutes of the time that was newly my own. I had just emancipated from the foster care system.

I took one last look around the dining room, thinking I was about to leave behind all the painful as well as funny incidents that had happened there. For the very last time, I pressed my hot palms on a wooden table that so many other palms had slapped or balled-up fists had pounded. I pushed the chair away with the back of my knees and stood up.

For months I had dreamed of this day and everything I would say to these people. I had comforted myself thinking they would no longer have the power to punish me for speaking my mind. But when the moment finally came for my speech, I simply said, "Well, it's been nice. I'll see you later."

Then I walked out the door, thinking I was shutting the gate of my hell behind me. I soon found out that those gates don't shut that easily. Just because you no longer live somewhere, doesn't mean you've left it behind.

Four hours later, I sat in the passenger seat of my friend's car—my new home—and read a card signed by my former counselors. "The world is now in your hands," one of them had scribbled. I laughed and threw the card aside.

For a long time I had been dreaming of my plans for that evening. My friend and I were going to drive from San Francisco to Ocean Beach, where I would burn a huge calendar that had every day crossed off—each square representing one day that I had survived group home life. Once the calendar turned to ashes, I would scream at the top of my lungs, "Free at last, thank God, I'm free at last!"

I couldn't simply "get over" my past, as people kept telling me to do.

But that was just another dream that didn't become a reality. Instead, I sat in the car, speechless and in shock, thinking how comfortable the group home's soft vinyl couch would be at this moment. My first few months in foster care I'd spent every day glued to that couch, sinking into a warm void. And now that was all I wished to do, when "the world was in my hands."

My friend had been in a group home herself, and seemed to have dealt successfully with the aftereffects of the experience. I wanted to know her secret formula for the cure.

But a cure for what? I didn't even know. Maybe the strange trance I had fallen into, where I no longer even had the energy to speak to people.

Perhaps I needed help with the fact that I had been weak and sensitive enough to have let group home life and all its hypocrisy play with my head—like the double whammy of being told by the staff to act like an adult, and then have them threaten to give me "consequences" whenever I tried to stand on my own two feet.

I learned that there were no cures, only painkillers. For months I consumed several joints a day, packs and packs of cigarettes, and enough beer to turn my skin golden. I stumbled late into the psychedelic renaissance. I went on an acid vacation, then feasted on mushrooms (including the dirt they came in) combined

There was nothing I could do to escape, except to start writing.

with pot. I laughed my butt off until I was afraid of laughing. For the first time in my life, I felt euphoria. But in the pursuit of happiness, I wiped out the money I had saved while at the group home—money I was supposed to use to find my own place.

I began to feel more desolate, but I didn't think it was a good idea to seclude myself from society. And so I went to bars and clubs, drank some more, met other people, and went crazy on the dance floor. I attempted to meet other "grown ups."

But there were no new friends to be made and no understanding from the old ones. There wasn't even pity, which at that moment I would have gladly picked up off the floor because of how low I had sunk. I couldn't fit in anywhere. People my age were too hip for some morbid fool, and the others, who were older, gave me cold looks of annoyance and disgust.

I tried going home to my mother's house, but that didn't

work for long. There was nowhere else to go but to live with my only friend in her car, where every day I lashed out at her, feeling that she, too, didn't understand what I was going through.

No matter where I went, I felt judged, alone, and angry. I couldn't simply "get over" my past, as people kept telling me to do. I began to have a small understanding of the Vietnam veterans who fought a losing cause, then returned home, stuck in their minds in the jungle forever, unable to deal with this other world.

Then one day my friend met up with a couple of her friends who had a house and agreed to help us out. After three months of sleeping in a car, my back was shooting pain and I was desperate for a shower.

For the next few months, I stayed with people who were con artists for a living and smoked crack as a hobby. Because I wasn't much of a talker, they called me a retard. I put up with it by smoking several eighths a day in three-inch thick joints.

I realized that I was going crazy. I didn't even dream anymore when I slept, and that scared the hell out of me. I began to grow unsure of myself. There was nothing I could do to escape, except to start writing down the events that had occurred at the group home. Those times still haunted me. I saw the facility in everything and everyone I encountered.

Looking for comfort, I began to call my former counselors, the ones I'd gotten along with. But, as one of them told me, her job with me was over and done: "It's time for us all to move on with our lives."

One day my primal scream erupted. I decked one of the people I was staying with, ripped out a handful of her hair, and waved it in her face as if it were a flag. I felt like a savage conqueror who had just stolen land.

In an instant, the woman's face had become that of the group home regional supervisor, and I screamed aloud out of fear and pride, "I got you, you $%^$@#!"

After that, I was homeless again, living in the car for another two months.

O ne day things took a turn. Writing became my new drug and my job. I even found a place to live. But every day I am still reminded of the time I spent in the grip of the foster care system.

Some time ago I went to a group home to teach a poetry workshop. I asked a counselor for a drink. She gave me an empty glass and proceeded to hand me a pitcher of water. I stood there, dumbfounded, until I realized that I was waiting for her to pour the drink for me. It was almost as if I were at home.

"The world is in your hands." I laugh. "Pursuit of happiness." I laugh. That calendar hides in my closet, an old souvenir.

"Deal with it," I hear over and over again from those who have never been system kids.

Don't you understand I'm trying to?

Hazel was 20 when she wrote this story for Youth Outlook
(Yo!), a youth newspaper in San Francisco.
Copyright © Yo!. Reprinted with permission.

Gary Smith / YC Art Dept.

My Brother Kareem

By Destiny Cox

My brother Kareem was my best friend for 10 years and 18 days—until the April day he was murdered.

Kareem's birthday was April 11. He was 14 years older than me, my mother's first child, but our birthdays were a day apart. (My birthday is April 10.) As an adult, he was about 6′ tall and wore glasses occasionally. He was light-skinned with thick eyebrows.

Growing up, mom said, Kareem loved to have fun. He was a great dancer and went to parties with friends from high school. He got into trouble sometimes, but never anything severe.

Since I was born premature, I had to stay in the hospital for a month. According to my mother, Kareem came to the hospital every day to see me until I got out.

Years later, he often picked me up from elementary school

and rode me home on his motorcycle. He'd circle around the block a couple times before we went home because he knew I loved the air I got each time he turned the corner.

After he parked his motorcycle and chained it up, he'd have me put the lock on the chain and touch it with my index finger. He said I gave it good luck.

Usually when we got upstairs, I didn't get my feet halfway through the door before he said, "Des, homework time." He did well in school and wanted me to do the same. I'd go through my homework once, then he'd go through it with me and correct my mistakes.

My brother had to deal with other responsibilities too. Kareem met his girlfriend April in high school and dated her for two years. Then, in her last year of high school, April got pregnant. My nephew Kareem Jr. was born when I was 5.

Kareem Jr. was eventually nicknamed Tink. He took away the attention my brother gave to me, and my brother and I started getting into spats. One day I started crying, and Kareem said, "Destiny, what's wrong with you?"

"Nothing," I said coldly.

"I know something's wrong," he said, sounding comical. "You have an attitude with me."

"Well, I don't appreciate you not spending that much time with me anymore," I said, still crying.

"Well, I have a son now, and I have to show him attention too," he said, drying my tears. "He's a baby. I showed you attention when you were a baby, right?"

"Yes," I admitted.

"OK then, you know I pay you attention, but from now on whenever I take Tink somewhere, I'll take you too," he said with a big smile. All I could do was laugh, because at this point he was tickling me like crazy.

Even though he had a son Kareem still lived with us, so I still saw him almost every day. He picked me up from school with

Tink sometimes. He was going to college and working, but hung out with me when he had time.

One Saturday night, my family was in a good mood because we had relatives visiting. I was even more elated because the next day Kareem planned to take me shopping.

I had been walking with him the week before and saw a denim dress that I wanted, so I asked for it for my birthday. "You're a spoiled brat and have big ears, but I guess I can get it for you," he said, pulling my ears out.

When he told me he would get it that Sunday, I was happy because I could wear it to school on Monday. So on Saturday, I was waiting for him to come from work at his construction site.

When he called Mom and told her that he wasn't going to work, I was happier. I thought that meant he'd come straight to our house. But I thought wrong. He told Mom he was going to a party.

I stayed by the door and waited for him to come home.

"Kareem, why are you going to a party with Todd?" Mom said. She was upset because my cousin Todd was a gang member. "He's only going to get you into some mess."

I don't know what Kareem said on the phone, but I did hear my mother say, "Be safe, Kareem."

After they finished talking to each other, she passed the phone to me. "Don't worry, Des, we're still going tomorrow to get your dress," Kareem said, before I even opened my mouth. He was reading my mind.

"What time will you be here?" I asked.

"I don't know, but I'll be there. Do I ever break promises?"

"Never," I replied.

"I'm happy you know that. I love you, Des."

"Love you too. Hurry up and dance, then come home."

Those were my last words to my older brother and best friend, Kareem Howerton Sr.

That night, I stayed at my aunt's house and hung out with my cousin Faith. The next morning I woke up to screams from the next room. Faith and I ran into the room to find my uncle holding my aunt. She looked like she was going to collapse.

"Why?" my aunt kept saying. "This cannot be."

"It'll be OK," my uncle kept telling her.

I kept asking what was wrong. "Destiny, we have to go to your house," my uncle said. "Get dressed." After we got dressed, Faith and I started to pray for Todd and Kareem because we had a feeling something had happened to them.

When I got to my house, my cousins, my grandma, and April were there. Mom was nowhere to be found. I asked Grandma where Mom was and she told me she went to the police precinct.

I thought she got arrested, so I asked what happened. Grandma said Mom was OK and that when she came back, she'd tell me what happened.

Out of nowhere, my uncle said, "Destiny, your brother is dead." I just looked at him with disbelief. Then it sunk in when everyone started to cry. Then I cried.

"This is not true," I said to myself.

My mother soon walked in. Her eyes were baggy and her face was red.

"Mommy, is Kareem really dead?" I said.

"Yes, sweetie," she said, with tears rolling down her face. I cried again, even harder this time. I ran to my grandmother and she hugged me tight.

Mom said the police told her that a fight had broken out at the party. A witness told the cops that it was between a friend of Todd's and another guy. Kareem tried to break up the fight, but Todd's friend was stabbed twice.

My brother tried to help him and pull him to his car. Then Kareem realized that he'd been stabbed also. He got to the car, but before he got his keys out, the guy ran out of the party and stabbed Kareem until he was unconscious. Then he ran away.

I couldn't believe Kareem was gone. I didn't want to think

about the reality of it. I wanted him to play with my ears and call me "big head." I wanted him to watch TV with me.

While my mother made funeral arrangements, I became isolated. I didn't go to school or outside much because I thought I should wait until Kareem's funeral services were over.

But I wanted to go outside. I wanted to continue to do normal things. I didn't want to do anything that made me believe that Kareem was dead. The first two nights after his death, I even stayed by the door and waited for him to come home. I was in deep denial.

So many people showed up at Kareem's funeral. There were two lines going around the corner of the block from the funeral home. Some people came up to me and gave me hugs and flowers. I was happy to see that so many people loved and appreciated Kareem.

Some teachers and students from my school came to his funeral too. They knew him from when he picked me up every day. Some of the boys looked up to him because he talked to them about going to school and how it would benefit them.

Writing became my window to let out the pain that I felt over Kareem's death.

During the service, I promised myself I wouldn't cry because so many people were crying and I wanted to be strong for everyone else, especially my mom. Even when I saw his body, I didn't cry. I hugged and kissed him in the casket.

But towards the end of the funeral, I broke down. I couldn't help it. Everyone was crying except me. It wasn't fair. At the gathering my family had after the funeral I felt a little better, probably because I'd gotten to say goodbye to Kareem.

A couple of days after the funeral, I returned to school. My grades soon started slipping fast. Instead of focusing on school, I thought about Kareem. My mother always told Kareem not to get involved with other people's messes, but he never listened. He was just a very caring person. She tried to talk to me about his death, but that didn't help much. I felt like no one could under-stand me, so I didn't want to talk.

She tried to help me feel better by buying me new toys and clothes, but that didn't help either. I was in my own world. I felt like my heart was getting smaller and smaller each day.

Living without Kareem was really hard. I always missed him when I was at the park next to my building because that's where he taught me how to ride my bike.

I soon turned to an old habit. When I was younger, I wrote things down that bothered me and often felt better as a result. So I adopted writing as a way to heal my grief.

I wrote letters and poetry about Kareem that usually explained how much I missed him and how much he meant to me. I also wrote about the good times I spent with him. Writing became my window to let out the pain that I felt over Kareem's death.

When I first started writing my poetry, I wrote things like "I can't believe my brother is gone…" or "Why did this have to happen to me?"

But I gradually began to accept my brother's death not just as a loss, but as a life experience. After three months of venting, I wrote things like, "Having my brother die has made me a stron-ger person."

A couple of my friends also helped me with Kareem's death by spending time with me when I was sad. I managed to pick up my grades by the end of the term. I realized that letting my grades slip wasn't helping matters. Even after I began to feel bet-ter, though, there were times that I felt sad and depressed.

Now I'm 16, and it's been six years since Kareem passed away. His case never made it to trial. We never found the man who killed him. There weren't enough witnesses willing to talk to the police.

Knowing that Kareem's murderer hasn't been found bothers me a lot. Sometimes I wish I could get revenge myself.

Obviously, I'm not totally over it, but I deal. When his birthday comes around, or during the holidays, I miss him deeply and wish he was in my presence. I cry a lot at those times and get depressed, and I know that'll continue to happen in the future.

My mother and I still don't talk about Kareem's death much. When she does talk about it, she gets emotional and cries, so I don't bring it up. But I feel that it could be helpful for us to talk about him to keep our memories of him alive.

Losing my brother has made me appreciate life more. Now I try to live every day to the fullest. I never know when I'm going to go.

Although I've always been a nice person, I'm nicer now to people who I don't even know. I show others what my brother showed me, and that makes me feel better about not having him around. It shows that I learned from him.

Kareem's passing has also helped me to cope with death better. When my grandmother passed away, I handled it a little bit better than my brother's death. I didn't cry as much and I talked about how I felt more with my family members.

I don't think of Kareem's death as a loss anymore because he's still with me spiritually. I count on him to bring me strength and to look out for me. I will always love my brother.

Destiny was 16 when she wrote this story. She later attended Delaware State University and joined the U.S. Navy.

Karolina Zaniesienko

In the Realm of Guilt and Sorrow

By Linda R. Rodriguez

Now I will dare to take you into the realm of guilt, of sorrow, of helplessness, of worthlessness, of an emotion that should be remedied with the soothing voice of a friend or the silence of a willing ear.

Now, if this emotion is ignored and kept in the closet or under the covers, it can be very deadly. One dose of this emotion can send the most rational person tumbling headfirst into the fifth dimension of insanity.

Depression.

The word didn't exist in my vocabulary at the time I was overwhelmed with it. I just thought I was very sad. I tried my hardest not to feel that sadness. In fact, I beat myself up anytime I even thought I was upset.

What I felt was guilt for having such sorrow and rage. I felt guilty for feeling the way I did while my mother loved me and showed her love by telling me stories, taking me places, buying me presents, teaching me all sorts of things. And I felt guilty for feeling so sad when my mother had troubles of her own.

My mother had me when she was just 16. My parents stayed married only long enough to have my brother, when I was 4 or 5. As I grew up, I learned to tiptoe around my family's frequent explosions.

At my father's mother's house, somebody was always bad-mouthing my mother. At home, my mother would use the same dirty words to describe my father's family. When the two sides got together, I was usually caught in the middle.

One night, for instance, when I was supposed to sleep over at my grandmother's house, my mother called. Angry words were exchanged and my mother said she was coming to pick me up.

When my mother got to the house I heard an explosion of profanities. From the window I watched my grandmother, mother, and aunts yelling in the street, and my tears just turned on like a faucet. I began to gather my things when my cousin grabbed my arm and told me, "Don't worry about it, she'll leave."

I said, "Look, she's not leaving without me. I'll just go now."

Then the cops pulled up and half the neighborhood came out in their pajamas to see what the commotion was about. That's when I descended the steps and got into my mother's van so the argument would be over.

I was always doing whatever I could to please my mother. The rare times I threw out hints to disagree with the bad things she said about my father's family, she'd accuse me of loving them more, or even of loving only them. This made me bawl like a baby (of course not in front of her). How could she question my love when I tried so hard to show her I loved her?

Sometimes her anger would escalate—usually after she'd

been drinking from her bottle of anger-inducing "medicine." One minute we'd be dancing at a party, celebrating, and the next she'd be tugging on my already thinning head of hair.

Often, I'd take the beatings and hurtful words as my fault. Although I'd fight with kids in school when anyone even thought of bothering me, I'd take whatever my mother gave out and try to be invisible.

My brother, on the other hand, was the "bad seed." He was always fighting with everyone, including my mom. Everywhere we went, someone was always telling me how bad he was.

I loved my brother to death. I mean we were allies in the war going on around us, but I blamed him for making our mom's life harder, and this caused our own battles.

Most of the time when my brother teased me I'd ignore him. I didn't want to be part of the hatred being casually thrown around. But when I couldn't take it anymore, I'd let every bit of rage my little body was holding explode through my fists of fury.

Once the fights started, they would go on for days and days. I guess both of us took advantage of them to let everything out while we could. When they ended, there was an atmosphere of bitter relief. But soon the tensions would begin to build again, and I'd tiptoe, again, around the land mines, paying no mind to all the negativity that was being compressed into my fragile little body.

When I was 10 or 11, though, I became overwhelmed with all my family's dysfunction and I was filled with a new wish, to be by God's side frolicking amongst the angels. I wanted to leave the earth because everything seemed so painful.

I wanted to die but I was afraid to kill myself. Instead, I prayed to God—"Take me already! You've taken kids younger than me." Or I'd fantasize about being caught in a gunfight. I would hear the explosion of gunpowder and feel my insides shatter.

I began to place myself in dangerous situations. I'd leave the protection of my mother's watch and go off into the park alone. I thought maybe I'd get lucky and someone would kill me.

Patience is not one of my strong points. I wanted to die right then, so one day I just said, "The hell with it, I'll do it." Everyone else caused me pain. Why shouldn't I?

The day I tried I felt like I was finally going to end all the hell. I was in the living room with my brother listening to music on the stereo real loud. We were dancing or maybe wrestling. My mother was in her room with her friends. The only light was the lava lamp with red wax bubbling up and down in its bottle prison.

My brother and I sat down on the sofa. I asked him, "What would you think if I killed myself?"

I remember the look on his face asking the silent question, "What are you talking about?"

I went and got my rainbow jump rope and tied it to my mother's exercise bar. I wasn't scared. At that point, I looked at suicide as if I were just walking out the front door. What I saw was the happiness I was sure to get if I escaped the madness.

I felt guilty for feeling so sad when my mother had troubles of her own.

I stepped up to the rope and wrapped it around my neck. Then I hung onto the bar like a monkey. I looked at my brother and asked, "Should I let go?"

I did let go a little. My eyes bulged and my head grew very warm. My little fingers were slipping.

"No!" my brother yelled. He took a giant step toward me and wrapped his arms around my waist. He lifted me away from the gravity that was pulling me to death.

I wrapped my arms around him, squeezing him, holding onto life. For the remainder of the night we sat, with the speakers pounding, in the red darkness, electrified and shushed at the same time. All the while my mother never even peeped out her bedroom door.

The colorful rope dangled from the exercise bar for a day or two before my mother noticed. Looking back, I think I left the rope up there because I wanted my mother to ask how I was doing.

I had figured I would just tell her I was playing Indiana Jones, but when she did ask, I told the truth.

She couldn't believe it. She held my shoulders with my arms pinned down as if I were going to fall from my own words. Seeing her upset in turn upset me, and my tears flowed.

The next dagger to her heart would have been if I told her how much she was hurting me. So I blamed it all on the petty fights I duked out with my brother. Even then I knew that was a pathetic cop out.

My mother took me to a therapist who asked me questions like, "What emotions do you feel most throughout the day? Do you tell anyone how you feel? Who makes you feel this way?"

I wanted help but I didn't want to let this stranger in. I gripped my slithering demon and pushed it down to my toes. I was determined never to let it out, because to talk was against my code. She suggested that I stay as an inpatient in the psychiatric ward.

I stayed in the hospital for two weeks. For me, my cornerless room—with its door wide open, with the cameras watching my every move, with the voice through the intercom in the middle of the night, with the nurse feeding me my happy pills—was a get-away from the world that made me try too hard and made me hurt too much.

I went to one-on-one therapy and group therapy with 10 other "suicidals." Still, I didn't want to let anyone into my emotional cave. I wanted them to help me from a distance. So instead I just gave them crumbs. I would tell them a little bit, then leave them with a million questions to answer for themselves.

The choice was ours to talk or just to sit there for the time allotted. Many times, silence was my better friend.

But during my quiet time in my un-private room, I began breaking down my own walls. Sitting on that crisply-made bed, with the therapists' questions floating in my head, I began to see that my family's constant conflicts had a lot to do with how I was feeling.

It wasn't easy to see. I'd been building my walls for so long that there were just so many layers blocking my vision. Besides, my walls were made of metal and brick. But as I allowed a little bit of those layers to be chipped away, my anger began to seep out.

The day I really let it out started with an innocent visit from my mother. I had made a special card to show her I was improving, but when we were left alone, once again I became the garbage can for her emotions. Mami said I was so stupid for needing to be in the hospital, while I sat quietly listening.

After the visit, I sat on my bed trying to suck back my tears. Then my sadness turned into the familiar rage. I looked around. This wasn't my room and this wasn't my home. I felt like I would never be home because my heart belonged nowhere.

I grabbed the card I'd made and ripped it into the tiniest pieces. When I was through, my floor looked like a bag of confetti had busted all over.

Next I stripped my mattress of its sheets and pillow. I threw them all in a messy pile on top of the bed and on top of it the stuffed animal my mother's boyfriend had bought for me. I wanted to rip that, too. I wanted to get rid of everything that had to do with my family.

Then one of the staff members walked in. I sat down on the bed with a smirk on my face, catching my breath, smoothing my hair. She said, "Why did you do this?"

I shrugged and sat there with the coolest mask. I was a pro.

"Well, you have to clean this mess up. You know that, right?"

"No," I spat.

"Why not? This is your room and you made the mess."

The next words slipped out unexpectedly, surprising us both. "'Cuz I don't feel like it. I'm not cleaning nothing."

She said she was going to put me in the rubber room for a time out. "I'm not going anywhere," I said. It was one of the first times I had ever talked back to an adult. It felt good, and also scary. Finally, I gave in and said, "Fine, let's go."

I was placed in a room that was all rubber, with a window that looked out onto a brick wall and a rubber ball in the middle to take your anger out on. Being in that room made me insane. I wanted to break the stupid ball, so I tried. When I couldn't, I tried to destroy the room.

I scuffed up the floor with my sneakers and tried to break the windows and walls. Then I just lay on the floor and started howling. I kept my howls loud and long.

I had begun to accept that there were real problems in my family, and that those problems were hurting me.

Someone opened the door and asked me if I was ready to come out. I just spit out my, "No." When the staff member closed the door I threw the ball at it and some more madness was released.

I was in there for a long while howling. Finally I calmed down and came out.

Afterward, while picking up those stupid little papers in my room, I thought about what I'd done. Usually, at least around adults, I knew how to be the nice, respectful, goody-goody girl. I was shocked that my rage had burst out of control, and that I had let it flow the same wild way my brother usually did. It made me discover the strength of my own feelings.

When my two weeks were up, my mother came and took me home. My stay at the hospital had spoiled me and I wanted to see that my mom cared as much about me as the people in the hospital did. When I didn't see that, and the fighting continued, all I knew was that I wanted to go back to the security I'd had there.

Instead, I learned how to numb myself again, but this time I tried to tune out everyone else's pain, too. My mottoes became, "I forgot," and "The hell with it." I just tried to enjoy my life.

Once in a while, for brief moments, I'd let the slithering demon out of me. We moved around a lot in my first year in high school, and I began to say, "Who cares what the kids in school know about me? I'm probably moving again." So while I was talking to some kid about basketball or whatever, I'd slip in a few heavy, personal tidbits.

Some of those kids became my friends, and the little bit that I let out made a difference. I didn't feel as alone as before. It was a beginning.

When I thought things were looking a little better, life as I knew it was crushed. My brother accused my mother of abuse. I guess he was tired of getting beaten all the time. As a result, I got separated from my family and put in the foster care system.

After my suicide attempt and my time spent in the hospital, I had begun to accept that there were real problems in my family, and that those problems were hurting me. But the fact that my family could be separated completely shocked me and threw me back into denial.

So instead of holding my mother responsible for beating us, I blamed my brother. Why did he have to be a punk and tattle on my mother?

I, on the other hand, would do anything I could to keep my family together. So I told the courts that my mother never beat us. Instead, I said she punished us in healthy ways to teach my brother and me some discipline. And I told myself that my mom wasn't so bad. She stretched her dollars for my brother and me, and she never let us forget that we were her reason for living. I thought that if I really believed what I said, somehow we would be able to stay together.

But that wasn't good enough for the courts and so they ruled that there would be no more Mami for me. Instead, I would be sent to New York to live with my maternal grandmother, who I'd seen a good five times in my life.

For the first few weeks that I was in New York, I slept all the time, trying to make the days go by quicker, knowing that tomorrow Mami would call for me to come back home. Even after I was enrolled in high school, I made no friends for several months because I believed that soon enough, it would be time for me to leave.

After a while I realized that I wasn't going home any time soon, but that didn't change things very much for me. School seemed pointless since I didn't have my family anymore to push me to work hard, and I started failing classes that I could easily have passed. I slept in most mornings and strolled over to school during my lunch period. I didn't want to try to do anything. I just wanted to find a way to go back to feeling numb.

Over that year, though, I began to realize that I didn't have the super-strength it took to make myself go numb on demand. I would break down whenever anything reminded me of my family, which was often, and tears would well up in my eyes.

And when the worst of my depression lifted, I began to watch how the other kids enjoyed interacting, and I didn't want to be the only sad sack anymore. I wanted to get rid of my endless depression. I didn't know how I was going to do that, but I was going to try.

I started out trying a little too hard (it was more like trying to forget.) By the summer, all those things that I didn't get myself into when I was younger became my pastimes. I started drinking, cutting school, and partying 'til my body couldn't take it anymore.

I also began to make my voice heard. I'd always respected adult authority, but I wasn't willing to give into their tyranny anymore. So when my grandmother would demand that I be home at a certain time, I would flat out defy her. I would yell, "Are you trying to insinuate that I'm out there smoking crack or prostituting or something? I go to the parties to dance and have fun." I'd flip the script on her and say, "Do you want me to be in the house all day like you?"

I knew I probably shouldn't talk to my grandmother like that, and it wasn't really her rules that bothered me. But it was easy to yell at her, because I never really knew my grandmother, so I felt liberated to speak my mind. And I was just so tired of my years of silent submission.

When I was out being wild and rebellious, I did feel better. At least I was out enjoying the life of a teen, asserting what I wanted and breaking free. But when I was home alone again, I would remember that I still had unsolved sadness. And I knew that if I didn't deal with the pain that was there, I would wake up a miserable old woman years from now, complaining about how life had screwed me over.

Dealing with that pain wasn't easy. It meant opening old wounds, and sometimes it felt like pouring salt on them, too. In the long run, though, it helped me to shake hands with the truth.

I didn't want to try to do anything. I just wanted to find a way to go back to feeling numb.

I had some help to get me started. When I came to New York, my grandmother hooked me up with a mental health program that worked out of my new high school. Having my therapist, Donna, in my school was convenient and gave me a reason to actually make every appointment (unless I cut school).

Donna was a pleasant person and earned a bit of my confidence by letting me know the rules straight off the bat. She let me know that it was my choice what I told her. She also let me know that everything I said was basically between her and me, and that she wasn't going to call in the snooperific authorities.

I was still suspicious, though. Besides, I didn't always want to deal with reality. As a result, I gave her some of the same flowery stories that I was used to recounting. Other times I'd tell her a little bit about what went on, but never the whole truth.

For instance, I admitted to Donna that my mother did hit me and my brother, which I hadn't admitted to an outsider before. But I would never tell her about the severity of the beatings. When she'd ask me more, I'd just say, "Yeah, she used to hit us on the butt."

And occasionally I'd tell her about some bad times, like one time that my mother spit some extremely foul language in my ear. But then I'd deny it was even a problem. I'd say, "Oh, that's just the way we did things."

Most of the time Donna would ask, "If everything was OK, then why did you attempt suicide?" It was that question that stuck in my head and it was that question that kept forcing my eyes open to reality.

After my sessions with Donna, I would feel an outburst lurking right under the surface (and only drinking could ease my mind). Donna was digging up all my feelings and it took a lot of effort for me to shove them back down.

So the next year, when the therapy program and Donna moved out of the school, I decided that I would make a change, too. It was only one stop on the subway from my school to see Donna, but I felt that if I made the effort to go that one more stop, it would be like admitting that Donna had influence over me. I was not willing to say that therapy was doing much of anything for me, so little by little I just stopped going.

After I left Donna, though, I began analyzing my problems for myself with the same questions that she had asked me. And without Donna there, there was less reason for me to lie about what had happened. I'd worked so hard to convince Donna that my stories were real, that in some ways I'd convinced myself. But when I was on my own, I had no good excuse to deny the truth. I didn't want to recycle the confusion in my own life or my children's lives. I wanted the vicious cycle to end with me.

So when I went out and got drunk or high or just partied all night, I began to question the reasons for my actions. On my way back home I would wonder what my life's final destination was going to be.

The flowery answers that I had given Donna were the foundation on which I built my analysis. I asked myself, "Why was I inclined to give those pretty stories?" and more so, "Why did I believe in them?" Sometimes I'd ask if it wasn't really better to believe my lies. But then I'd feel the sadness and anger inside me, and my answer would be no.

After a while, I admitted to myself that my mother wasn't the best in the world. I loved her, but beating me while she was in an alcoholic blackout wasn't the best parenting technique. And yes, her life was hard, but maybe she could have kept a little bit of her sorrows to herself or at least waited until I was older. As a little child, I'd had to take on more than I could handle.

I'd started to accept that when I'd been in the hospital, but going into foster care had forced all that honesty out of me.

When I was out being wild and rebellious, I did feel better. But when I was home alone again, I would remember that I still had unsolved sadness.

When I began to accept those things again, I also started to realize that I couldn't control everything that happened around me. I wasn't responsible for or capable of making everything just peachy. When I was younger, I had taken all my family's emotional baggage and believed that I could resolve their issues. That I couldn't was one of the major reasons for my depression.

I began to say, "All right, my family doesn't get along. If I've done all I can to help them and they still have conflicts, that is where I have to leave the issue. I can't control their world. I only have control over one thing, which is my life and me."

That helped me calm down and get more in control. I started to be less wild than I used to be. For several years I wasn't a very good student, but now I've successfully finished one semester of college. I am the product of my environment and I can't deny it, but I'm learning to construct instead of destruct.

I still get depressed sometimes, but I know how to deal with it a little better now, which includes looking the reasons for my depression in the face. It was actually during a bout of depression that I was inspired to write this story.

A couple of months ago I got a call from my mother. She said my brother was in trouble and had been threatening to take his own life. I felt desperate to get in contact with him. That old urge to save my family returned to me. Then I found out that a friend was looking to make her own ending because she felt so truly alone. I gave a try at counseling her, but I felt like my words only went so far. Then another of my close friends was entertaining the idea of not existing. What was I supposed to do and what was I supposed to think?

That's when I decided to write my own story. I hope it helps my friends and my brother a little when they want to walk out that door, like I once almost did.

Linda was 18 when she wrote this story.
She later attended Lehman College.

Julieth Riano

What Is Depression?

By Anonymous

After I wrote about being depressed, I wanted to know more about it, and about how to help a friend who might be feeling alone like I was. So I interviewed Dr. Alexandra Barzvi, a psychologist at the New York University Child Study Center.

Q: What is depression and how do you know if you have it?

A: Sometimes what we tend to call depression isn't really depression. Many teenagers feel blue and moody at times. If it passes in a few days to a week, there's nothing to be concerned about.

Clinical depression is diagnosed when a teen experiences a depressed or irritable mood and/or a loss of interest and pleasure in almost all activities, for at least two weeks.

You might be depressed if a really positive event doesn't cheer you up. Also, be aware of your eating and sleeping patterns. If you're suddenly having a hard time sleeping, or find that you're eating a lot more or a lot less, it might be time to talk to someone.

Q: How long can depression last and can it go away on its own?

A: Untreated major depression can last months or even years. Depression can also come and go in cycles, with periods of relief followed by a reoccurrence.

The "blues" are normal and likely to fade with time or a change in routine. Major depression is not likely to go away without treatment. No one can "will" themselves not to feel depressed.

Q: What kind of treatment is available for depression?

A: Nearly two-thirds of depressed teens don't get proper treatment. Those who do are treated with either therapy, medication, or a combination of the two.

If the depression is severe, medication is often recommended. Research has shown that one kind of therapy that works is cognitive-behavioral therapy (CBT) in combination with medication. A major aim of CBT is to change the beliefs or behaviors that help to keep the depression going. Everyone has thoughts that "automatically" pop into their heads, but depressed teens tend to have more negative ones.

The first step in controlling our negative thoughts is to learn to become aware of them and to identify the ones we have most often.

Q: Why might a teenager refuse to talk to someone about feeling depressed?

A: Depression can be hard to talk about. Some teens have a difficult time putting words to their feelings.

If you know someone who might be depressed, try to listen without trying to fix them. The more accepting you are, the more they're likely to tell you. But remember, it's not your responsibility to understand exactly what your friend is going through.

Q: How can you help a friend who is depressed?

A: Depression plays tricks on people, making them see themselves, other people and the world in a negative way. Your friend's perspective on life might be foggy and instead of looking forward to the future, your friend might be feeling hopeless and helpless.

Take your friend's comments seriously and don't try to convince them not to feel bad. Ask them what might be helpful, but don't promise to keep the information secret. Encourage your friend to get help, but if they don't, tell someone that you are worried. Don't assume someone else is handling the problem. But don't make it your problem either. Ask for help from your parents, teachers or guidance counselors.

The writer was in high school when she
conducted this interview.

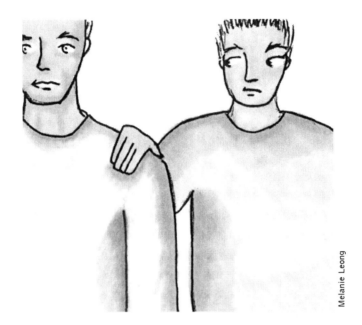

Melanie Leong

How to Help a Friend in Need

By Anonymous

When I look at my friends, I see the people I've known for so many years and who I confide in. I also see a group of screwed up kids who have been through so much: relationships that ended badly, school problems, and depression.

Last year I watched a friend get really down and stop acting like the person I'd known for years. He even tried to OD. What's up with that? Why are so many teens feeling alone and angry? And what can other teens do to help their friends?

I really wanted to know the answers to those questions, so I turned to a couple of social workers who work with young people.

John Pettinato, a former social worker who is the principal of Institute for Collaborative Education, explained that three of the most common signs of depression are not doing well in school, major problems with parents/guardians, and drug use.

Other signs are smaller and harder to notice, like seeming unresponsive or particularly quiet, sleeping too much or having insomnia, eating too much or too little, and being angry or sad for what seems like no reason.

Pettinato said teens tend to "act out" their issues, meaning that if they're angry, it can lead to violent outbursts, or if they're sad, they may have random crying fits. They may not even know what's wrong.

Some withdraw, while others don't care anymore about things they liked to do. If you see your friend change and show warning signs like these, your friend might need to get help.

If you think a friend is hurting, there are several ways to help. You can just show him you care and encourage him to open up to you. "When a person is having difficulty, they need their friends," Pettinato said.

By spending time with a friend and really talking with him, you can help him figure out what's getting him down. Just showing you care and will listen can help. Teenagers especially are more likely to listen to a friend's point of view before anyone else's.

Just showing you care and will listen can help.

"Teens, by definition, feel alienated. Leaving them alone only justifies those feelings," Pettinato said.

Pettinato also recommends what he called an "intervention," which is when a group of people discusses someone's problem with them.

For example, if you think a friend is feeling down, you can tell him that you've noticed a change in him and you're concerned. Tell the person what changes you've seen, and ask what's behind them. Remind your friend that you're available if he needs to talk.

You want to talk in a comfortable environment and take care not to be judgmental. You don't want to make the person feel he's done something wrong.

Unfortunately, your friend may not open up. Many teenagers are either afraid or unwilling to tell adults about their problems. Gary Mallon, who teaches at the Columbia University School of Social Work in New York City, explained that young males are taught by society not to ask for help.

"From when they're little kids, they're always told, 'Be a man,' " he said. "They're expected to handle their own problems because that's what men do. It makes it difficult to talk to adults about what's bothering them."

Mr. Mallon pointed out how, in many families, communication is strained and awkward, because teens are

'If your friend tells you more than you can handle, you should refer him to a professional for help.'

unwilling to share their feelings. Also, many teens, young males especially, mistrust adults, turning to friends instead. But other teens often don't know how to handle their friends' serious problems.

For example, when my friend tried to OD and then told me about it, I didn't do anything because I felt overwhelmed.

Pettinato said that any time a person may be in danger of hurting himself or others, you should always speak up. When my friend told me he tried to OD, "it was his way of telling you he was so needy he might have killed himself. In that situation, you definitely should've told a professional," Pettinato said.

Mallon suggested that friends refer teens in trouble to school counselors, hotlines, or professionals like social workers and psychologists.

"If your friend tells you more than you can handle, you should refer him to a professional for help," Mallon said. He encouraged teens to seek help for themselves if they don't feel they're getting enough support.

"When you feel you've gone as far as you can with your support network of friends and family, like if they feel they can't help you, or they're tired of hearing what you have to say, or if they just say they don't know what to do, you need to turn to a professional," he said.

The writer was 18 when he wrote this story.
He later graduated from college and went to law school.

Patricia Battles

Flipping the Script

By Hattie Rice

"Listen to the beat," says Melissa, wincing at the sight of my dancing. "Now lean with it."

"Damn, how is it I'm black and I ain't got no rhythm? Ain't that supposed to be a given?"

"Sometimes I wonder about you," Melissa says, sarcastically. "Let's keep it simple, to just the snap."

I try to snap and end up like a white person putting up the crip sign (it just won't work).

I zone out in thought: "Why am I so slow? Lord Jesus, why don't I get it? How stupid can one person be? It's just a snap. Then again, Lord Jesus can't help me, even with the Twelve Apostles. Why try? Is it really going to help? I can be quite the dummy."

That's the type of thing I say about myself at least three times a day—until I take a deep breath and repeat the following words:

"OK, I'm not that slow." Then I exhale all the negative energy.

Whenever I try something new, I feel very discouraged. I always think things are going to go wrong, maybe because in the past many things have. For instance, I liked my group home and was comfortable there. Did I think that was going to last? No! And it didn't. I was shipped off to a foster home. People predicted the foster home would be good and I said it would be bad. Guess who was right?

After years of disappointments, I don't have confidence that anything will have a positive outcome. I predict things will go wrong so that when they do, I'm not surprised. It's a way of getting used to the many shortcomings in my life and protecting myself from getting let down.

I also constantly tell myself that I'm dumb, so that insults from others don't hurt too badly. That started when teachers, kids at school, and even my family teased me and called me names. Repeating those taunts to myself lessened the pain I felt when I heard them from others.

Although these are good strategies for handling disappointments, I recently realized that they're also holding me back from fully enjoying my life. I don't get excited about new experiences because I fear they'll go wrong. And I don't feel as much pride and joy about what I do well because I'm bracing myself for the good times to go bad.

These days, my life is a lot more stable than it once was. I'm living in a better foster home, coming up on high school graduation, and already accepted to a good college—SUNY Binghamton in upstate New York. I don't need to brace myself for failure anymore.

I need to work on my pessimistic attitude so I don't prevent myself from growing and living my life to the fullest. I hope to act more positive, enjoy things, and attract positive people to me. I want to learn to accept the compliments people give me without using skepticism or sarcasm to downplay what they've said. And

I want to stop beating myself up.

So this past winter I joined the Transitions Workshop, a 14-week group where teenagers learned new coping mechanisms (we called them "tools") to help us get through difficult changes. I chose to work on changing the negative script in my head and stop putting myself down.

Each week of the workshop we had to try a new "tool," and then report back to the group on how it went. We also kept diaries of our journeys. Here is my diary of my attempts to change how I think about myself:

March 16

This week I decided to keep tabs on myself and write down how often I criticize myself and what I say. Surprisingly, I found out I don't criticize myself as often as I thought, but when I do I'm really harsh. It's like, why do I need enemies when I've got myself? It shouldn't be that way.

As a way to motivate myself to eliminate the problem, I decided to write down a reminder of why I need to make this change. I realized I've never been on a roller coaster or ridden a bike, and I can't swim or snap my fingers—all because I've never really tried. It was painful to face how much I am holding myself back.

If I complete this change I may learn how to do all those things, maybe even whistle. Those are the little things, but they're steps toward my overall goal of building more confidence in myself and my abilities. My writing was a wake-up call that my constant self-criticism is not only crippling my self-esteem, but also damaging my ability to try new things.

March 23

This week I wrote some more about my problem—this time writing down some of the terrible criticisms I heard as a child from classmates, like: "Why you sitting here talking to the quiet fool?" or "I can't even sit next to her. Yo, shorty a straight weirdo."

I was shocked to remember that a girl in my class had the audacity to talk about me to my face. But writing down those insults surprised me because my feelings were less intense than I thought they would be, which was good. I even reread what I wrote, which I never do.

My journal writing left me in such good spirits that I decided on the first action I would take to change. I decided that for the rest of the week I'd tell myself good things whenever something negative happened.

I need to work on my pessimistic attitude so I don't prevent myself from living my life to the fullest.

Trying this technique also surprised me because it somewhat worked. If I started to criticize myself, I was able to stop it and tell myself good things

The problem was I didn't believe a word that was coming out of my mouth. I truly felt like a compulsive liar, and a bad one at that. Despite telling myself all these good things, I still felt incompetent deep down. But I think that I need to program my first thought to be positive, and eventually my feelings about myself might catch up.

April 6

Continuing with my theme of telling myself positive things, I planned this week to put post-its on my mirror with my positive characteristics written on each. That way, I'll wake up each morning with good feelings about myself and I'll be able to study my positive qualities. I also wrote an on-the-go list of my positive qualities in my journal so I'd always have it with me.

The list included: introspective, intelligent, considerate, understanding, timid, intuitive, intricate, broad minded, caring, and able to disregard my emotions during times of stress.

I decided that I'd take a quiz about what's good about me. I know that may sound weird, but the best way to get an idea fixated into my brain is to study. I studied the list as if for a real test, and I kept repeating it to myself randomly. Sporadically during the day I would think, "I'm beautiful and an intellectual."

This plan was good because it helped me look in the mirror (which I hardly ever do). I'm definitely going to make this a routine.

Despite my list, I had a hard time when we discussed "self-esteem" in health class. It brought me back to my lowest moments of childhood. I kept remembering unpleasant memories that made me feel bad about myself. At least saying positive things about myself helped get my mind off those past memories.

April 13

This week I chose to write a story about a time in my life when I used all the positive characteristics I posted on my mirror. The story was a way to remind myself of my strength.

Here's what I wrote:

"When I was at home with my mom, she refused to talk to me. In fact, she refused to talk to any of her family. (She has schizophrenia and was addicted to crack for years.) Everyone else left her alone and ignored her crying.

Although I was only 12, I was intelligent and intuitive enough to realize that my mom wasn't OK and needed help expressing herself. So instead of going to school, I was considerate and sensitive of her feelings—I stayed at home with her every day.

I wasn't sad to miss school. When I was younger, going to school was painful because I only had two outfits, my skin looked horrible, and my mom would mess up my hair. So you can imagine how much I got teased. (I am amazed that I go to school today.)

That year I stayed home I was patient. I knew of my mom's violent nature, so I waited and eventually she opened up to me. She told me how she felt watched, and she pulled the blinds down. She told me that a boyfriend she had when she was 10 hypnotized her and was now having her watched. She claimed my father was in on it, telling 'Casper' of her whereabouts.

As far fetched as the story was, I listened and did not interrupt. The story was unreal, but her pain was not. The situation made me feel strong yet scared. It was good that my mom had me to turn to, but who did I have?

Soon after that I was placed in foster care. I am involved with my family but remain detached emotionally, so I am able to live and not let their needs consume me. I still visit them, to show them my loyalty and let them know that they are irreplaceable."

Writing all of this down, I reminded myself of my strength and resilience. It was good to remember that there are reasons I have trouble feeling positive about my life, but also that the worst times are behind me.

April 20

This week I meant to "seek social support"—surround myself with friends—because one thing I don't think I do well is communicate with new people. Because of the criticism I've experienced and the way I criticize myself, I usually believe that others won't like me.

I meant to hold a sleepover, but that didn't work out, so instead I went on a college tour with my friend Natasha. It went very well. I talked to kids on the bus, and Tasha and I talked to some college kids all by ourselves. We then finished off the day by going to my house and just chilling. I found out that I can communicate when I want to, if I'm around someone I like.

It was painful to face how much I am holding myself back.

I also read a book called *The Joy of Doing Things Badly* by Veronica Chambers. The book helped me realize that I should focus on making myself happy, because I owe myself more of my attention than I owe anybody else.

Veronica wrote about doing what you enjoy, even if you do it by yourself, and explained that you'll feel more confident if you surround yourself with what makes you feel good. Her book was a reminder to me that I'm not going to do everything well, and

I don't need to criticize myself just because it takes time to learn new things.

April 27

While participating in the workshop and writing this story, I've uncovered some interesting things about myself. I've realized that I'm stronger than I thought I was. I feel inspired to work on other aspects of my life that bother me. Maybe it is possible for me to be happier day to day.

Sometimes the group was stressful. But I also learned that I could participate in an intense group without freezing up or isolating myself. I bonded with the other teens and, for the first time, I had a strong social circle. That's helped me realize that people aren't going to criticize me if I let them in. I can communicate with people, and I can try to deal with my worst struggles.

Throughout the weeks of the workshop, I thought negatively about my planned tools and then found out they were effective at making me feel better. As it turns out, there are alternative ways I can approach the problems I'm facing, rather than simply writing about them.

Even though the workshop is over, I plan to continue to write letters to myself because they help me express my inner anger, and to put words on my mirror, which help me recognize my inner beauty. I've realized that being pessimistic takes joy from my life, and trying to be more positive has been a change worth making.

Hattie was 17 when she wrote this story.
She later attended SUNY Binghamton.

Townsend Press

Lost and Found

Darcy Wills winced at the loud rap music coming from her sister's room.

> My rhymes were rockin'
> MC's were droppin'
> People shoutin' and hip-hoppin'
> Step to me and you'll be inferior
> 'Cause I'm your lyrical superior.

Darcy went to Grandma's room. The darkened room smelled of lilac perfume, Grandma's favorite, but since her stroke Grandma did not notice it, or much of anything.

"Bye, Grandma," Darcy whispered from the doorway. "I'm going to school now."

Just then, the music from Jamee's room cut off, and Jamee rushed into the hallway.

The teen characters in the Bluford novels, a fiction series by Townsend Press, struggle with many of the same difficult issues as the writers in this book. Here's the first chapter from *Lost and Found*, by Anne Schraff, the first book in the series. In this novel, high school sophomore Darcy contends with the return of her long-absent father, the troubling behavior of her younger sister Jamee, and the beginning of her first relationship.

"Like she even hears you," Jamee said as she passed Darcy. Just two years younger than Darcy, Jamee was in eighth grade, though she looked older.

"It's still nice to talk to her. Sometimes she understands. You want to pretend she's not here or something?"

"She's not," Jamee said, grabbing her backpack.

"Did you study for your math test?" Darcy asked. Mom was an emergency room nurse who worked rotating shifts. Most of the time, Mom was too tired to pay much attention to the girls' schoolwork. So Darcy tried to keep track of Jamee.

"Mind your own business," Jamee snapped.

"You got two D's on your last report card," Darcy scolded. "You wanna flunk?" Darcy did not want to sound like a nagging parent, but Jamee wasn't doing her best. Maybe she couldn't make A's like Darcy, but she could do better.

Jamee stomped out of the apartment, slamming the door behind her. "Mom's trying to get some rest!" Darcy yelled. "Do you have to be so selfish?" But Jamee was already gone, and the apartment was suddenly quiet.

Darcy loved her sister. Once, they had been good friends. But now all Jamee cared about was her new group of rowdy friends. They leaned on cars outside of school and turned up rap music on their boom boxes until the street seemed to tremble like an earthquake. Jamee had even stopped hanging out with her old friend Alisha Wrobel, something she used to do every weekend.

Darcy went back into the living room, where her mother sat in the recliner sipping coffee. "I'll be home at 2:30, Mom," Darcy said. Mom smiled faintly. She was tired, always tired. And lately she was worried too. The hospital where she worked was cutting staff. It seemed each day fewer people were expected to do more work. It was like trying to climb a mountain that keeps getting taller as you go. Mom was forty-four, but just yesterday she said, "I'm like an old car that's run out of warranty, baby. You know what happens then. Old car is ready for the junk heap. Well, maybe that hospital is gonna tell me one of these days—'Mattie Mae Wills, we don't need you anymore. We can get somebody younger and cheaper.'"

"Mom, you're not old at all," Darcy had said, but they were only words, empty words. They could not erase the dark, weary lines from beneath her mother's eyes.

Darcy headed down the street toward Bluford High School. It was not a terrible neighborhood they lived in; it just was not good. Many front yards were not cared for. Debris—fast food wrappers, plastic bags, old newspapers—blew around and piled against fences and curbs. Darcy hated that. Sometimes she and other kids from school spent Saturday mornings cleaning up, but it seemed a losing battle. Now, as she walked, she tried to focus on small spots of beauty along the way. Mrs. Walker's pink and white roses bobbed proudly in the morning breeze. The Hustons' rock garden was carefully designed around a wooden windmill.

As she neared Bluford, Darcy thought about the science project that her biology teacher, Ms. Reed, was assigning. Darcy was doing hers on tidal pools. She was looking forward to visiting a real tidal pool, taking pictures, and doing research. Today, Ms. Reed would be dividing the students into teams of two. Darcy wanted to be paired with her close friend, Brisana Meeks. They were both excellent students, a cut above most kids at Bluford, Darcy thought.

"Today, we are forming project teams so that each student can gain something valuable from the other," Ms. Reed said as Darcy sat at her desk. Ms. Reed was a tall, stately woman who reminded Darcy of the Statue of Liberty. She would have been a perfect model for the statue if Lady Liberty had been a black woman. She never would have been called pretty, but it was possible she might have been called a handsome woman. "For this assignment, each of you will be working with someone you've never worked with before."

Darcy was worried. If she was not teamed with Brisana,

maybe she would be teamed with some really dumb student who would pull her down. Darcy was a little ashamed of herself for thinking that way. Grandma used to say that all flowers are equal, but different. The simple daisy was just as lovely as the prize rose. But still Darcy did not want to be paired with some weak partner who would lower her grade.

"Darcy Wills will be teamed with Tarah Carson," Ms. Reed announced.

Darcy gasped. Not Tarah! Not that big, chunky girl with the brassy voice who squeezed herself into tight skirts and wore lime green or hot pink satin tops and cheap jewelry. Not Tarah who hung out with Cooper Hodden, that loser who was barely hanging on to his football eligibility. Darcy had heard that Cooper had been left back once or twice and even got his driver's license as a sophomore. Darcy's face felt hot with anger. Why was Ms. Reed doing this?

Hakeem Randall, a handsome, shy boy who sat in the back row, was teamed with the class blabbermouth, LaShawn Appleby. Darcy had a secret crush on Hakeem since freshman year. So far she had only shared this with her diary, never with another living soul.

It was almost as though Ms. Reed was playing some devilish game. Darcy glanced at Tarah, who was smiling broadly. Tarah had an enormous smile, and her teeth contrasted harshly with her dark red lipstick. "Great," Darcy muttered under her breath.

Ms. Reed ord e red the teams to meet so they could begin to plan their projects.

As she sat down by Tarah, Darcy was instantly sickened by a syrupy-sweet odor.

She must have doused herself with cheap perfume this morning , Darcy thought.

"Hey, girl," Tarah said. "Well, don't you look down in the mouth. What's got you lookin' that way?"

It was hard for Darcy to meet new people, especially someone like Tarah, a person Aunt Charlotte would call "low class." These were people who were loud and rude. They drank too much, used drugs, got into fights and ruined the neighborhood. They yelled ugly insults at people, even at their friends. Darcy did not actually know that Tarah did anything like this personally, but she seemed like the type who did.

"I just didn't think you'd be interested in tidal pools," Darcy explained.

Tarah slammed her big hand on the desk, making her gold bracelets jangle like ice cubes in a glass, and laughed. Darcy had never heard a mule bray, but she was sure it made exactly the same sound. Then Tarah leaned close and whispered, "Girl, I don't know a tidal pool from a fool. Ms. Reed stuck us together to mess with our heads, you hear what I'm sayin'?"

"Maybe we could switch to other partners," Darcy said nervously.

A big smile spread slowly over Tarah's face. "Nah, I think I'm gonna enjoy this. You're always sittin' here like a princess collecting your A's. Now you gotta work with a regular person, so you better loosen up, girl!"

Darcy felt as if her teeth were glued to her tongue. She fumbled in her bag for her outline of the project. It all seemed like a horrible joke now. She and Tarah Carson standing knee-deep in the muck of a tidal pool!

"Worms live there, don't they?" Tarah asked, twisting a big gold ring on her chubby finger.

"Yeah, I guess," Darcy replied.

"Big green worms," Tarah continued. "So if you get your feet stuck in the bottom of that old tidal pool, and you can't get out, do the worms crawl up your clothes?"

Darcy ignored the remark. "I'd like for us to go there soon, you know, look around."

"My boyfriend, Cooper, he goes down to the ocean all the time. He can take us. He says he's seen these fiddler crabs. They look like big spiders, and they'll try to bite your toes off. Cooper says so," Tarah said.

"Stop being silly," Darcy shot back. "If you' re not even going to be serious . . . "

"You think you're better than me, don't you?" Tarah suddenly growled.

"I never said—" Darcy blurted.

"You don't have to say it, girl. It's in your eyes. You think I'm a low-life and you're something special. Well, I got more friends than you got fingers and toes together. You got no friends, and everybody laughs at you behind your back. Know what the word on you is? Darcy Wills give you the chills."

Just then, the bell rang, and Darcy was glad for the excuse to turn away from Tarah, to hide the hot tears welling in her eyes. She quickly rushed from the classroom, relieved that school was over. Darcy did not think she could bear to sit through another class just now.

Darcy headed down the long street towards home. She did not like Tarah. Maybe it was wrong, but it was true. Still, Tarah's brutal words hurt. Even stupid, awful people might tell you the truth about yourself. And Darcy did not have any real friends, except for Brisana. Maybe the other kids were mocking her behind her back. Darcy was very slender, not as shapely as many of the other girls. She remembered the time when Cooper Hodden was hanging in front of the deli with his friends, and he yelled as Darcy went by, "Hey, is that really a female there? Sure don't look like it. Looks more like an old broomstick with hair. " His companions laughed rudely, and Darcy had walked a little faster.

A terrible thought clawed at Darcy. Maybe she was the loser, not Tarah. Tarah was always hanging with a bunch of kids, laughing and joking. She would go down the hall to the lockers and greetings would come from everywhere. "Hey, Tarah!" "What's up, Tar?" "See ya at lunch, girl." When Darcy went to the lockers, there was dead silence.

Darcy usually glanced into stores on her way home from school. She enjoyed looking at the trays of chicken feet and pork ears at the little Asian grocery store. Sometimes she would even steal a glance at the diners sitting by the picture window at the Golden Grill Restaurant. But today she stared straight ahead, her shoulders drooping.

If this had happened last year, she would have gone directly to Grandma's house, a block from where Darcy lived. How many times had Darcy and Jamee run to Grandma's, eaten applesauce cookies, drunk cider, and poured out their troubles to Grandma. Somehow, their problems would always dissolve in the warmth of her love and wisdom. But now Grandma was a frail figure in the corner of their apartment, saying little. And what little she did say made less and less sense.

Darcy was usually the first one home. The minute she got there, Mom left for the hospital to take the 3:00 to 11:00 shift in the ER. By the time Mom finished her paperwork at the hospital, she would be lucky to be home again by midnight. After Mom left, Darcy went to Grandma's room to give her the malted nutrition drink that the doctor ordered her to have three times a day.

"Want to drink your chocolate malt, Grandma?" Darcy asked, pulling up a chair beside Grandma's bed.

Grandma was sitting up, and her eyes were open. "No. I'm not hungry," she said listlessly. She always said that.

"You need to drink your malt, Grandma," Darcy insisted, gently putting the straw between the pinched lips.

Grandma sucked the malt slowly. "Grandma, nobody likes me at school," Darcy said. She did not expect any response. But there was a strange comfort in telling Grandma anyway. "Everybody laughs at me. It's because I'm shy and maybe stuck-up, too, I guess. But I don't mean to be. Stuck-up, I mean. Maybe I'm weird. I could be weird, I guess. I could be like Aunt Charlotte . . ." Tears rolled down Darcy's cheeks. Her heart ached with loneliness. There was nobody to talk to anymore, nobody who had time to listen, nobody who understood.

Grandma blinked and pushed the straw away. Her eyes brightened as they did now and then. "You are a wonderful girl. Everybody knows that," Grandma said in an almost normal voice. It happened like that sometimes. It was like being in the middle of a dark storm and having the clouds part, revealing a patch of clear, sunlit blue. For just a few precious minutes, Grandma was bright-eyed and saying normal things.

"Oh, Grandma, I'm so lonely," Darcy cried, pressing her head against Grandma's small shoulder.

"You were such a beautiful baby," Grandma said, stroking her hair." 'That one is going to shine like the morning star.' That's what I told your Mama. 'That child is going to shine like the morning star.' Tell me, Angelcake, is your daddy home yet?"

Darcy straightened. "Not yet." Her heart pounded so hard, she could feel it thumping in her chest. Darcy's father had not been home in five years.

"Well, tell him to see me when he gets home. I want him to buy you that blue dress you liked in the store window. That's for you, Angelcake. Tell him I've got money. My social security came, you know. I have money for the blue dress," Grandma said, her eyes slipping shut.

Just then, Darcy heard the apartment door slam. Jamee had come home. Now she stood in the hall, her hands belligerently on her hips. "Are you talking to Grandma again?" Jamee demanded.

"She was talking like normal," Darcy said. "Sometimes she does. You know she does."

"That is so stupid," Jamee snapped. "She never says anything right anymore. Not anything!" Jamee's voice trembled.

Darcy got up quickly and set down the can of malted milk. She ran to Jamee and put her arms around her sister. "Jamee, I know you're hurting too."

"Oh, don't be stupid," Jamee protested, but Darcy hugged her more tightly, and in a few seconds Jamee was crying. "She was the best thing in this stupid house," Jamee cried. "Why'd she have to go?"

"She didn't go," Darcy said. "Not really."

"She did! She did!" Jamee sobbed. She struggled free of Darcy, ran to her room, and slammed the door. In a minute, Darcy heard the bone-rattling sound of rap music.

Want to read more? This and other *Bluford Series*™ novels and paperbacks can be purchased for $1 each at www.townsendpress.com.

A Guide to Getting Help

It can be frustrating to need help for emotional or mental health problems and not understand what kind of help is available or where to find it.

This guide is designed to help you get the services that are best for you. It covers some typical issues for which teens seek help. It also briefly describes the kinds of people who provide help. And it describes the type of help they provide and the ways they provide it. After reading this guide you may have more questions. Talk with friends and with an adult you trust.

How Do I Know If I Need Help?

When people have a fever or a cold, they have a *physical* problem. Similarly, when people frequently feel sad, find it difficult to concentrate in school, or feel overwhelmed by life's daily problems, they have what is called an *emotional* problem. As with physical problems, emotional problems can be mild, such as occasional sadness, or severe, such as weeks or months of feeling low.

Just as some physical illnesses or injuries can be addressed through rest or physical therapy, emotional problems can be addressed through self-help, counseling, and various kinds of therapy. Emotional problems, like physical problems, can also be treated with medication. Some kinds of medication can help balance your body chemistry to help you feel more in control of your feelings—somewhat like how other drugs can attack germs and help restore the balance needed for physical health.

So how do you know when to seek help for an emotional problem?

We can try to answer this question by looking at depression. That's the name people often use to describe everything from occasional sad moods to a serious disease requiring medical treatment. People who are depressed can feel sad, discouraged, and hopeless. They can feel irritable, lose interest and pleasure in daily activities, and feel worthless and alone. They can feel very angry.

Many people experience these feelings from time to time. However, if you have those kinds of feelings for weeks or months on end—and if they make it hard for you to get out of bed in the morning, go out in public, enjoy eating, socialize with friends, or participate in other activities you think you really should be enjoying—you need to seek therapy (more on therapy below). The feelings will not just go away by themselves.

Even mild depression can lead to thoughts of suicide and actual suicide attempts. Again, many people have occasional thoughts of suicide when they are very upset, such as after breaking up with a boyfriend or girlfriend. But if you continue to think about hurting yourself and are planning ways to end your life, you must tell someone and get professional help. If you won't tell an adult, tell a peer. Start sharing your feelings with a trusted friend if this is easier for you.

But you don't have to be depressed or feel suicidal to seek help. There are many other problems that can affect your ability to function and be happy. You may have feelings of loneliness, anxiety, or isolation. Perhaps you have conflicts with parents, siblings, or friends, or maybe someone in your family is suffering from mental or physical illness. Maybe you can't concentrate enough in school to do as well as you know you can.

If you have a problem that is interfering with your ability to feel productive or deal with the daily ups and downs of life, your best option is to connect with someone who can help.

Who Can Help Me? How Do I Know What Kind of Help Is Best For Me?

Professional therapy is not the only kind of help out there. In the next few paragraphs we'll briefly describe some other ways you can seek help for an emotional problem. Even if you're going to therapy, knowing how to use these other supports can be helpful. We start with the most informal kinds of counseling you can get, and work up to the most formal or specialized.

Help yourself. First, there's **self-help**. Self-help means what it sounds like. You help yourself, often without any counselor at all. If you feel sad or angry because you're shy and can't make friends, and you read a book or magazine article on how to be less shy, and you feel happier because it works, you're doing great. There's probably no need to go to a counselor.

If you're upset, you can try writing down your feelings in a journal and describing the circumstances that are causing you to feel that way. Writing can help you release feelings that are bottled up and may help you see things differently and find solutions to your problem.

Get help from peers. The next level is getting help from friends. There are two main ways to do that: informal help from people you know, and something more formal called **peer self-help.**

Informal help from your friends means talking to friends about your problems. If you're feeling lonely, angry, or sad, confiding in a friend can help you feel better (as it helped many of the writers in this book). You probably already know that, and already do it. Again, friends can help up to a certain point: if you feel the problem is serious, you many need more help than your friends can give.

Peer self-help is a more formal way of getting help from people like you. It usually happens in groups. The groups are often run (or "facilitated") by an adult professional, but the real benefit comes from other teens in the group. So, for example, if you are cutting and want to stop, you might be able to find a self-help group of teens whose problems led them to cut themselves. They get together regularly to talk about problems in their lives and what strategies they use to try to stop cutting.

Get help from community members. There are lots of people in your day-to-day life who may be helpful to you. They might include **school counselors, teachers, clergy, coaches, mentors,**

and any other adult who you trust and feel comfortable talking to about your problems. Some of them, like a minister, may have some training in counseling. Others, like a mentor, may not. But you're a good judge of how comfortable you are talking to them. If you start to feel better after talking with them, great. If not, they may be able to recommend someone else who could be helpful. Remember, it may take more than one talk session to help you feel better about yourself and your life, so give yourself and your counselor a chance.

Get help from professionals. Therapists are professionals who are specially trained to help people with mental health issues. A therapist may be a psychiatrist, a psychologist, or a social worker. The main difference is that psychiatrists are medical doctors, which means they can prescribe drugs.

But whatever their training and background, most therapists do pretty much the same thing. They listen closely to how you describe what's making you feel bad. Then they work with you to help you change the thinking or feelings or actions that cause you problems or pain.

When They Say I Need Therapy or Counseling, What Do They Mean? What Kinds Are Available?

Counseling is a process where people explore their feelings, behavior, and what's going on in their lives. People go to counseling because they want to find ways to feel better and be more effective in their lives. (This kind of counseling is often called **therapy** or **psychotherapy**, or **psychological counseling** to show that it's different from something like job counseling.) If you get into formal counseling or therapy, you'll probably experience **individual counseling, group counseling,** or **family counseling,** or perhaps all of them. If your problems are severe, you may be **hospitalized.** We briefly describe these options below.

Individual Counseling: In individual counseling or therapy, you meet one-on-one with a counselor, usually at his or her office. You usually meet regularly, at least once a week, for any-where from a few months to a year or longer, depending on the issues you're working on. You play an active role in defining the goals of your therapy with your counselor.

Group Counseling: In group counseling, a group of people who share common problems, concerns, and questions meet reg-ularly to discuss feelings, and to listen to and support each other. For example, people who have lost loved ones may participate in bereavement groups. The groups are often (but not always) led by a mental health professional. Groups are also common in drug treatment programs. Everyone in the group has a drug problem, and the groups are often led by people who have their addictions under control, and who are especially skilled at working with people with drug problems.

Peer self-help groups are one kind of group counseling, and they exist for many, many issues. Alateen is a peer self-help group for teens who have family members with alcohol prob-lems. There are peer groups for teen parents, teens with eating problems, teens who've lost a loved one, and for teens with many other issues.

Family Counseling: In family counseling, two or more mem-bers of a family will meet together and separately with a coun-selor to discuss conflicts, issues, and communication in the fam-ily. The counselor helps the family members deal with important issues without taking sides.

Hospitalization: If you have severe emotional or mental health problems, such as strong feelings of hopelessness or that you may hurt yourself or someone else, or that you're losing con-trol, or that you cannot quit drugs without more structure and support, you may want to be hospitalized or referred to a drug rehab center. Hospitalization (which is also called "in-patient" treatment because you stay in the hospital) gives you a chance to get intensive services. For example, you may participate in indi-vidual, group, family, or peer counseling every day, as well as be given medication, to see what helps you most.

What If I Feel Uncomfortable in Therapy?

One goal of therapy is to help you solve some problems, and to think differently about the problems you can't solve, so you can better manage how they affect you. When that happens, your self-esteem usually starts to rise. However, it can be very uncomfortable to look at problems in your life.

If you begin to feel uncomfortable in therapy, or feel that you are not making progress, don't just jump to another therapist. Discuss these issues with your therapist. A good therapist should be willing to talk with you about treatment issues, and about whether the therapy is meeting your needs. A good therapist should also be willing to consider changing the way he or she works with you.

It is usually a bad idea to make a snap decision concerning your therapist. It is important in therapy to gradually face hard issues about yourself or others in your life. That can be very difficult. Sometimes the *best* therapist is the one who is demanding and sometimes even makes you feel pretty uncomfortable. The times that you want "out" of therapy or feel you need another therapist may be when you're making the most progress. At those times, it can be hard to figure out whether you don't like the *therapist*, or whether you don't like the *issues* he or she is asking you to think about. You need to be able to trust that your therapist has your best interests at heart, even if he or she sometimes makes you feel uncomfortable.

It takes time to develop trust in a new relationship and to comfortably share feelings, so give your therapist and yourself some time. But if you've given it an honest shot and still don't feel you can trust your therapist, or if you don't feel like you're making progress over time, you may need a change.

Can I Change Therapists?

Who you see for help should depend most on who you feel comfortable with and who is being most helpful to you. If you start with a therapist and either feel uncomfortable or feel that you are not making progress, or you are prescribed medication and don't want it, you need to discuss these issues with your therapist. Together you can decide whether it would be best for you to see another therapist or whether you need more time to work together.

It can be helpful, before starting therapy, to check out more than one therapist. If it's possible for you to do so, meet with two or three therapists, ask them how they work, and try to get a sense of how comfortable you feel with each.

But it may not be possible for you to "shop around." For example, you may be assigned a therapist. Yet even if you are assigned a therapist, you can ask to be changed to a new one if, after working together for a time, you feel that person is not right for you.

Privacy

When you talk with someone about your private issues, you probably don't want them sharing that information without your permission. It's a good idea to ask the therapist in your first session what sort of confidentiality he or she can provide. For example, will the therapist share your conversations with your parents? With other people in the agency? Will the therapist share some kinds of information, but not others?

In general, people who offer licensed psychological counseling (psychiatrists, psychologists, and social workers) can offer much more confidentiality than informal counselors, like teachers and mentors (who may not be legally required to keep your conversations confidential). You need to ask them who they share information with and why—and then make your own decisions about what you want revealed to your parents and other concerned persons.

Note that even if everything else you say is confidential, therapists are obligated to tell others if you threaten to harm yourself or others.

A Word About "Cognitive-Behavioral" Therapy

In addition to the forms of therapy described here (individual counseling, family counseling, etc.) there are many *kinds* of therapy. One kind that has been shown to work well with teens for some issues is cognitive-behavioral therapy. That's a fancy name for a pretty simple technique.

"Cognitive" means "thinking." In the first part of cognitive-behavioral therapy you work to replace self-defeating or self-destructive thoughts with more helpful thoughts. For example, if you're failing in school, you may think, "I'm sure to fail every class." But if you can change your *thinking* to, "I failed because I didn't study," and, "If I study for my next test, I may do better," then you're half way there to a good change.

But just changing your thinking isn't enough. You also have to change your behavior—what you do. In the example about failing classes, if you change your *behavior* too (that is, you actually do some studying)—then things will start to change for the better.

Therapists who use cognitive-behavioral methods help support you in changing negative thinking and actions into more positive approaches.

A Word About Medication

Just as doctors prescribe medication to treat physical illness, doctors also sometimes prescribe medication to treat emotional problems, such as depression.

There is medication for all kinds of emotional problems, but the most common ones for which teens get medication include depression, having trouble focusing (ADD, ADHD), and severe acting out or uncontrolled behavior (ODD).

One medication may be effective for some people but not for others. For example, many people use anti-depressants and feel the medication changed their lives by lifting their depression. But there are others for whom the medication has not worked as well. For teens, there's another issue. Studies show that for 2 or 3 teens out of 100 taking anti-depressants may actually make them feel more suicidal.

Also, if it is suggested that you take medication, you may wonder if it's because medication is cheaper than "talk therapy." Or maybe the clinic hasn't taken enough time to really evaluate you and they seem be jumping to the conclusion that you need medication. Or *you* may feel it is easier to take medication than to talk about your problems, so you go along, even though it might not seem like the best thing.

That's why you need to ask questions, and discuss your concerns with your therapist when you start any therapy program, especially one that involves medication. Medication may be necessary and very effective, but you and your therapist need to give careful thought to whether you need them.

And then, over time you, your therapist (and the psychiatrist who prescribed the medication) will evaluate the effectiveness of the drug and make changes until you figure out what works best. Your input will be very important because you are the only one who really knows how it is affecting you.

It is important to take medication exactly as prescribed, and then to notice how it makes you feel. If it doesn't seem to be working or has unpleasant side effects—or makes you feel suicidal—you may need to be put on another medication or need a smaller dose, or go off medication altogether. But since getting the right medication and the right dose to reduce your symptoms is complicated, it is very important that you work closely with your therapist and assigned psychiatrist.

You need to play an active role in coming up with a treatment plan with your therapist that works for you and then monitoring the plan and how it is affecting you.

Remember, some problems can be treated by self-help and

informal counseling with adults you trust. But for other problems you may need help from therapists and sometimes from medication, or even hospitalization. Don't be afraid to seek help if you feel you need it. Seeking help early may prevent problems from becoming more severe.

Teens:
How to Get More Out of This Book

Self-help: The teens who wrote the stories in this book did so because they hope that telling their stories will help readers who are facing similar challenges. They want you to know that you are not alone, and that taking specific steps can help you manage or overcome very difficult situations. They've done their best to be clear about the actions that worked for them so you can see if they'll work for you.

Our teen writers also helped put together the "Guide to Getting Help" on p. 118. This guide explains what kind of help is out there for teens dealing with emotional problems, and how to get what you need.

Resources on the Web

We will occasionally post Think About It questions on our website, www.youthcomm.org, to accompany stories in this and other Youth Communication books. We try out the questions with teens and post the ones they like best. Many teens report that writing answers to those questions in a journal is very helpful.

How to Use This Book in Staff Training

Staff say that reading these stories gives them greater insight into what teens are thinking and feeling, and new strategies for working with them. You can help the staff you work with by using these stories as case studies.

Select one story to read in the group, and ask staff to identify and discuss the main issue facing the teen. There may be disagreement about this, based on the background and experience of staff. That is fine. One point of the exercise is that teens have complex lives and needs. Adults can probably be more effective if they don't focus too narrowly and can see several dimensions of their clients.

Ask staff: What issues or feelings does the story provoke in them? What kind of help do they think the teen wants? What interventions are likely to be most promising? Least effective? Why? How would you build trust with the teen writer? How have other adults failed the teen, and how might that affect his or her willingness to accept help? What other resources would be helpful to this teen, such as peer support, a mentor, counseling, family therapy, etc.

Resources on the Web

From time to time we will post Think About It questions on our website, www.youthcomm.org, to accompany stories in this and other Youth Communication books. We try out the questions with teens and post the ones that they find most effective. We'll also post lesson for some of the stories. Adults can use the questions and lessons in workshops.

Discussion Guide

Teachers and Staff:
How to Use This Book in Groups

When working with teens individually or in groups, using these stories can help young people face difficult issues in a way that feels safe to them. That's because talking about the issues in the stories usually feels safer to teens than talking about those same issues in their own lives. Addressing issues through the stories allows for some personal distance; they hit close to home, but not too close. Talking about them opens up a safe place for reflection. As teens gain confidence talking about the issues in the stories, they usually become more comfortable talking about those issues in their own lives.

Below are general questions that can help you lead discussions about the stories, which help teens and staff reflect on the issues in their own work and lives. In most cases you can read a story and conduct a discussion in one 45-minute session. Teens are usually happy to read the stories aloud, with each teen reading a paragraph or two. (Allow teens to pass if they don't want to read.) It takes 10-15 minutes to read a story straight through. However, it is often more effective to let workshop participants make comments and discuss the story as you go along. The workshop leader may even want to annotate her copy of the story beforehand with key questions.

If teens read the story ahead of time or silently, it's good to break the ice with a few questions that get everyone on the same page: Who is the main character? How old is she? What happened to her? How did she respond? Etc. Another good starting question is: "What stood out for you in the story?" Go around the room and let each person briefly mention one thing.

Then move on to open-ended questions, which encourage participants to think more deeply about what the writers were feeling, the choices they faced, and they actions they took. There are no right or wrong answers to the open-ended questions. Open-ended questions encourage participants to think about how the themes, emotions and choices in the stories relate to their own lives. Here are some examples of open-ended questions that we have found to be effective. You can use variations of these questions with almost any story in this book.

—What main problem or challenge did the writer face?

—What choices did the teen have in trying to deal with the problem?

—Which way of dealing with the problem was most effective for the teen? Why?

—What strengths, skills, or resources did the teen use to address the challenge?

—If you were in the writer's shoes, what would you have done?

—What could adults have done better to help this young person?

—What have you learned by reading this story that you didn't know before?

—What, if anything, will you do differently after reading this story?

—What surprised you in this story?

—Do you have a different view of this issue, or see a different way of dealing with it, after reading this story? Why or why not?

Credits

The stories in this book originally appeared in the following Youth Communication publications:

"Fighting the Monster Inside Me," by Alina Serrano, *New Youth Connections*, November 1999

"Clean and Kind of Sober," by Antwaun Garcia, *Represent*, May/June 2005

"How Can You Mend a Broken Heart?" by Magda Czubak, *New Youth Connections*, March 1995

"Starting Over Without Them" by Hattie Rice, *Represent*, March/April 2004

"Out of the Shadows," *New Youth Connections*, March 2009

"Brotherly Love," by Jeremiyah Spears, *Represent*, July/August 2000

"Dealing with Death," by Griffin Kinard, *Represent*, November/December 2006

"How to Cope With Life's Losses," by Shameeka Dowling, *New Youth Connections*, April 2008

"Worn Down," by Anonymous, *New Youth Connections*, May/June 2000

"The World in My Head," by Natasha S., *Represent*, September/October 2007

"Dealing With It," by Hazel Tesoro, *Represent*, May/June 2000

"My Brother Kareem," by Destiny Cox, *New Youth Connections*, November 2002

"In the Realm of Guilt and Sorrow," by Linda Rodriguez, *Represent*, March/April 2001

"What Is Depression?" by Anonymous, *New Youth Connections*, March 2007

"How to Help a Friend in Need," by Anonymous, *New Youth Connections*, May/June 2000

"Flipping the Script" by Hattie Rice, *Represent*, September/October 2006

About
Youth Communication

Youth Communication, founded in 1980, is a nonprofit youth development program located in New York City whose mission is to teach writing, journalism, and leadership skills. The teenagers we train become writers for our websites and books and for two print magazines, *New Youth Connections*, a general-interest youth magazine, and *Represent*, a magazine by and for young people in foster care.

Each year, up to 100 young people participate in Youth Communication's school-year and summer journalism workshops where they work under the direction of full-time professional editors. Most are African American, Latino, or Asian, and many are recent immigrants. The opportunity to reach their peers with accurate portrayals of their lives and important self-help information motivates the young writers to create powerful stories.

Our goal is to run a strong youth development program in which teens produce high quality stories that inform and inspire their peers. Doing so requires us to be sensitive to the complicated lives and emotions of the teen participants while also providing an intellectually rigorous experience. We achieve that goal in the writing/teaching/editing relationship, which is the core of our program.

Our teaching and editorial process begins with discussions

between adult editors and the teen staff. In those meetings, the teens and the editors work together to identify the most important issues in the teens' lives and to figure out how those issues can be turned into stories that will resonate with teen readers.

Once story topics are chosen, students begin the process of crafting their stories. For a personal story, that means revisiting events in one's past to understand their significance for the future. For a commentary, it means developing a logical and persuasive point of view. For a reported story, it means gathering information through research and interviews. Students look inward and outward as they try to make sense of their experiences and the world around them and find the points of intersection between personal and social concerns. That process can take a few weeks or a few months. Stories frequently go through ten or more drafts as students work under the guidance of their editors, the way any professional writer does.

Many of the students who walk through our doors have uneven skills, as a result of poor education, living under extremely stressful conditions, or coming from homes where English is a second language. Yet, to complete their stories, students must successfully perform a wide range of activities, including writing and rewriting, reading, discussion, reflection, research, interviewing, and typing. They must work as members of a team and they must accept individual responsibility. They learn to provide constructive criticism, and to accept it. They engage in explorations of truthfulness, fairness, and accuracy. They meet deadlines. They must develop the audacity to believe that they have something important to say and the humility to recognize that saying it well is not a process of instant gratification. Rather, it usually requires a long, hard struggle through many discussions and much rewriting.

It would be impossible to teach these skills and dispositions as separate, disconnected topics, like grammar, ethics, or assertiveness. However, we find that students make rapid progress when they are learning skills in the context of an inquiry that is personally significant to them and that will benefit their peers.

When teens publish their stories—in *New Youth Connections* and *Represent*, on the web, and in other publications—they reach tens of thousands of teen and adult readers. Teachers, counselors, social workers, and other adults circulate the stories to young people in their classes and out-of-school youth programs. Adults tell us that teens in their programs—including many who are ordinarily resistant to reading—clamor for the stories. Teen readers report that the stories give them information they can't get anywhere else, and inspire them to reflect on their lives and open lines of communication with adults.

Writers usually participate in our program for one semester, though some stay much longer. Years later, many of them report that working here was a turning point in their lives—that it helped them acquire the confidence and skills that they needed for success in college and careers. Scores of our graduates have overcome tremendous obstacles to become journalists, writers, and novelists. They include National Book Award finalist Edwidge Danticat, novelist Ernesto Quinonez, writer Veronica Chambers and *New York Times* reporter Rachel Swarns. Hundreds more are working in law, business, and other careers. Many are teachers, principals, and youth workers, and several have started nonprofit youth programs themselves and work as mentors—helping another generation of young people develop their skills and find their voices.

Youth Communication is a nonprofit educational corporation. Contributions are gratefully accepted and are tax deductible to the fullest extent of the law.

To make a contribution, or for information about our publications and programs, including our catalog of over 100 books and curricula for hard-to-reach teens, see www.youthcomm.org

About The Editors

Al Desetta has been an editor of Youth Communication's two teen magazines, *Foster Care Youth United* (now known as *Represent*) and *New Youth Connections*. He was also an instructor in Youth Communication's juvenile prison writing program. In 1991, he became the organization's first director of teacher development, working with high school teachers to help them produce better writers and student publications.

Prior to working at Youth Communication, Desetta directed environmental education projects in New York City public high schools and worked as a reporter.

He has a master's degree in English literature from City College of the City University of New York and a bachelor's degree from the State University of New York at Binghamton, and he was a Revson Fellow at Columbia University for the 1990-91 academic year.

He is the editor of many books, including several other Youth Communication anthologies: *The Heart Knows Something Different: Teenage Voices from the Foster Care System*, *The Struggle to Be Strong*, and *The Courage to Be Yourself*. He is currently a freelance editor.

Keith Hefner co-founded Youth Communication in 1980 and has directed it ever since. He is the recipient of the Luther P. Jackson Education Award from the New York Association of Black Journalists and a MacArthur Fellowship. He was also a Revson Fellow at Columbia University.

Laura Longhine is the editorial director at Youth Communication. She edited *Represent*, Youth Communication's magazine by and for youth in foster care, for three years, and has written for a variety of publications. She has a BA in English from Tufts University and an MS in Journalism from Columbia University.

More Helpful Books
From Youth Comunication

 *The Struggle to Be Strong: True Stories by Teens About Overcoming Tough Times.* Foreword by Veronica Chambers. Help young people identify and build on their own strengths with 30 personal stories about resiliency. (Free Spirit)

Fighting the Monster: Teens Write About Confronting Emotional Challenges and Getting Help. Introduction by Dr. Francine Cournos. Teens write about their struggle to achieve emotional well-being. Topics include: Cutting, depression, bereavement, substance abuse, and more. (Youth Communication)

 My Secret Addiction: Teens Write About Cutting. These true accounts of cutting, or self-mutilation, offer a window into the personal and family situations that lead to this secret habit, and show how teens can get the help they need. (Youth Communication)

Enjoy the Moment: Teens Write About Dealing With Stress. Help decrease the levels of stress in your teens' lives. These young writers describe how they cope with stress, using methods including meditation, journal writing, and exercise. (Youth Communication)

 The Fury Inside: Teens Write About Anger. Help teens manage their anger. These writers explore the causes of their anger and show how they gained better control of their emotions. (Youth Communication)

Analyze This: Teens Write About Therapy. Get insight into how therapy looks from a teen's perspective and help teens find the services they need. Teens write about their experiences with therapy. Some are happy with the help, while others are dissatisfied or confused. (Youth Communication)

Out of the Shadows: Teens Write About Surviving Sexual Abuse. Help teens feel less alone and more hopeful about overcoming the trauma of sexual abuse. This collection includes first-person accounts by male and female survivors grappling with fear, shame, and guilt. (Youth Communication)

Putting the Pieces Together Again: Teens Write About Surviving Rape. These stories show how teens have coped with the nightmare experience of rape and taken steps toward recovery. (Youth Communication)

Sticks and Stones: Teens Write About Bullying. Shed light on bullying, as told from the perspectives of the bully, the victim, and the witness. These stories show why bullying occurs, the harm it causes, and how it might be prevented. (Youth Communication)

Out With It: Gay and Straight Teens Write About Homosexuality. Break stereotypes and provide support with this unflinching look at gay life from a teen's perspective. With a focus on urban youth, this book also includes several heterosexual teens' transformative experiences with gay peers. (Youth Communication)

To order these and other books, go to:
www.youthcomm.org
or call 212-279-0708 x115

CPSIA information can be obtained at www.ICGtesting.com
Printed in the USA
BVOW04s0718011113

335183BV00008B/133/P

9 781933 939797